A COMPOSITE GOSPEL

A COMPOSITE GOSPEL

by

FRED L. FISHER
PROFESSOR OF BIBLE
HARDIN SIMMONS UNIVERSITY
ABILENE, TEXAS

Broadman Press
Nashville, Tennessee

PRINTED_IN THE UNITED STATES OF AMERICA
2.5AT527

Dedicated
to
Leah G. Fisher
my wife

CONTENTS

FOREWORD

People who desire to know Jesus and his message welcome every aid to that end. Such an aid is this work on the Four Gospels. Each Gospel presents Jesus from a different point of view in line with the definite purpose of the writer. In order to see Jesus completely, one needs to look at all four accounts at one time. This volume makes it possible for that to be done. The book is not a harmony, but employs all the principles of gospel harmony and strives to follow a correct chronology. The main value of the work, however, is found in its presentation of the deeds and teachings of Jesus as they appear in the Four Gospels but without repeating them in separate Gospel accounts. There is a real advantage gained at this point. Frequently a Gospel account of a statement leaves the impression that something is lacking, and a glance at the account in another Gospel reveals the thing which appears to be lacking. A combination of the two, or three, is likely the solution to correctness at the point of what Jesus did or said.

I have for many years felt the need for such a work as this. In it is found a splendid basic text for a course in the life and teachings of Jesus. Such a study, combined with projects in individual Gospel approaches, can be of untold value to those who are seeking to come to a knowledge of the truth concerning this important part of divine revelation. Students of Greek will find here a dependable translation from the original combined with mechanical devices to make the meaning evident upon the first reading. Students of New Testament criticism will follow with interest and profit the principles of harmony and evaluation set out by the author.

Unanimity of opinion can hardly be expected in such a work. Even a casual reading of a half dozen translations of the New Testament will indicate the truth so often expressed, "A translation is an interpretation." One of the aims of translation is that of bringing from the Greek text what Jesus meant in order that we may understand what he said. The reader of this volume should bear in mind that the writer has rendered no translation arbitrarily. Every phrase is a translation which results from close study of the original text from all the viewpoints of historico-critical translation: lexical, grammatical, syntactical, comparative. This same principle holds true in problems of chronology. The chronology here may differ from that which one has previously held. Fair appraisal of the chronology employed is desirable before final judgment is passed by the reader.

This is a day when a new interest in Jesus and what he has to offer to the world is being evidenced on every hand. This fact makes the book a timely work. Its value as an aid to understanding the life and teachings of Jesus will be limited only by the use made of it by students of religion.

RAY SUMMERS
Professor of New Testament Interpretation
Southwestern Baptist Theological Seminary
Fort Worth, Texas

INTRODUCTION

The central thing in the Christian religion is not a creed that has been formulated by man, nor a set of customs that has been adopted by man, nor a group of ceremonies that has come to be practiced by man, but a Person who has been revealed to man. The central thing in the Christian religion is Christ. It is this fact which invests the Gospel records with such tremendous significance for the Christian scholar. For in these records we have the story of the revelation of the Lord Jesus Christ. It is this record as found in the Four Gospels which gives us the clearest insight into the thought, intention, and ministry of our Lord. It is by this record that the truth of every subsequent book or doctrine or command must be tested.

The aim of this work is to furnish a supplementary help to the study of this record as it is found in the four canonical Gospels, Matthew, Mark, Luke, and John. My effort is to bring into one continuous story all that is found in the Four Gospels concerning Christ, to arrange this material in its proper chronological order, and to blend it together into one story formulated in modern English, based on an original translation of the Greek text.

It is hoped that this work will find a ready audience among three differing groups: First, college and seminary classes studying the life of Christ. Formerly such classes have found it necessary to use a harmony of the Gospels which sets the material in the Four Gospels in parallel columns. This is, of course, a helpful way of study and in some ways is of more merit than a work such as this, but it is hoped that this combination of the Gospels into one framework will prove even more helpful. Second, various church groups which are making a study of the life of Christ or of one of the Gospel accounts may find this work helpful in coming to a clearer understanding of the facts concerning the life and teachings of Jesus. Third, it is hoped that Christians will find in this volume a new kind

of life of Christ for devotional study and meditation. Instead
of retelling the story in my own words, I have sought to let
the evangelists who found such appreciative acceptance by the
early Christians tell the story in their own words.

It is not my purpose to try to supplant the Four Gospels
at all. Such an undertaking would be in vain. These Gospels,
presenting the gospel of Christ as they do from their individual
viewpoints, must always remain the cornerstone of Christian
teaching. It is rather to be hoped that this work will form a
valuable supplement to the study and understanding of the
story of Jesus.

In putting forth this work, there are certain basic assumptions which have been made. The scope of the work does not
permit the detailed argument of these questions, but I am not
completely ignorant of the problems involved and have tried
to come to an unbiased opinion in the light of a careful study
of all the evidence. My conclusion is that the evidence which
has been produced by centuries of Christian scholarship is
overwhelmingly in favor of the assumptions adopted.

First, I have assumed that the Four Gospels are the production of the apostles or of the companions of apostles who had
ample opportunity to know the facts of the ministry of Jesus.
They are not the imaginative products of some second century
writers who sought to justify their religious faith by an invented Jesus of Nazareth. This assumption means that the
material which we have in the Four Gospels may be accepted
as trustworthy. While everything which is known is not included, it may safely be expected that what is included has the
value of an eyewitness account of the words and deeds of our
Lord.

Second, I have assumed that the material which we have
in the Gospels is historically reliable. While it is freely admitted, yea, insisted upon, that the Gospels are religious books
written for religious purposes, it is also felt by this writer that
they are historically accurate. Their religious purpose—the
winning of heart loyalty to Jesus Christ—was best accomplished

xii

by the simple presentation of the facts about Jesus. His life did not need to be colored up in order to make it appealing.

On the basis of these assumptions this work is projected, and in its projection four tasks have been undertaken which I will now try to explain.

DETERMINATION OF THE AUTHENTIC TEXT

The first task was to determine the authentic text of the Four Gospels. The scope of the work did not include a minute study of the text nor a full presentation of all the textual evidence. The conclusions of modern scholarship are trustworthy at this point. For the most part I have depended on these conclusions. The Greek text of Westcott and Hort has been taken as basic for this work. With this has been compared, when textual questions arose, the text of Nestle's *Greek New Testament*. Also, when a real problem of translation was involved, the various critical apparatus of critical commentaries was consulted, and footnotes give the reason for my decision when I found it necessary to depart from the text of Westcott and Hort. Happily for this work, some of the most vexing textual questions are solved by combining all four of the Gospels. The text which is questioned in one Gospel is often authentic in another. Take as an example of this the formula with which Jesus gave the cup to his disciples when he instituted the Lord's Supper (Mark 14:24; Matthew 26:28; Luke 22:20). Many ancient authorities leave out the word "new" in the texts of Mark and Matthew. Therefore, in them, this is a questionable reading. In Luke, however, this is undoubtedly a part of the original text. Its inclusion in Matthew and Mark is probably due to the familiarity of some copyist with the text of Luke. So the complete formula is: "This is my blood of the new covenant which is shed for many for the remission of sins." All of this is based on an authentic text in one of the Four Gospels. On the basis of textual evidence, it has been found necessary to omit two paragraphs of material: John 7:53 to 8:11 and Mark 16:9-20. Neither of these passages contains any teaching which is contrary to the spirit of the New Testament or which would impair the Gospels, but it is now almost universally accepted that neither passage is a part of the original text.

The Blending of the Accounts

The second major task involved the blending of the Four Gospels into one account. The aim was to include a full account of each event—as full as possible in view of the Gospel material—and to repeat nothing except what it is probable that Jesus himself repeated. In doing this, I dealt only with sections of material. It is entirely probable that Jesus often repeated sayings and performed similar works during his ministry. No effort has been made to do away with these or to combine sections that are not true duplications. Our work included only the blending of various accounts of the same event or saying. The value of this is seen in the formula mentioned. Luke tells us that his blood was shed for "you"—the immediate group of the disciples—and that it constitutes a new covenant. Mark tells us that the blood was shed for "many," which is equivalent to saying that it is universally efficacious. Neither he nor Matthew identifies this covenant with the new covenant in their texts. Matthew adds the information that this shedding of blood is definitely related to the remission of sins. None of the accounts gives a complete interpretation of the meaning of the blood. Taken together, however, they do give a complete interpretation: "This is my blood of the new covenant which is shed for many for the remission of sins." Thus we see that the various accounts supplement one another and when taken together give a more complete account of the words and works of Jesus.

Translation of the Text into English

The third major task involved in this work was the translation of the text into English. The aim was to give a smooth, readable, simple, and accurate translation which would carry over the meaning of the Greek text into English. Of course, this is more easily said than done. I only hope for some meas-

ure of success in it. Certain principles of translation were
formulated and followed as closely as possible. These included:
(1) translate as accurately as possible the meaning of the original text; (2) give the translation in modern terminology where
it is possible to do so without changing the meaning of the
account—terms of measure, value, etc., were given in modern
American terms, but terms such as "reclining at the table"
were retained because they picture a custom of the day; "thee
and thou" were retained in direct address to God;[1] and "Christ"
is uniformly translated "Messiah"; (3) shorten idiomatic
Greek expressions which become tautological in English, such
as "he answered and said"; (4) translate only those particles
which are necessary to give the meaning of the Greek—such
expressions as "and," "but," "also," and "for" often make poor
English and add nothing to the translation; and (5) arrange
the translated material in accordance with modern usage, with
one exception: quotation marks are omitted and direct quotation is introduced by a capital. It was thought that these
principles were safe and sound in arriving at an acceptable
translation of the Greek text. I gladly acknowledge my in-
debtedness to the many fine translations of the New Testament
into modern English. My translation was compared with
them with every effort to avoid plagiarism. The appearance
of the Revised Standard Version of the New Testament in
the course of this work gave another valuable translation with
which to compare my conclusions.

ARRANGEMENT OF THE MATERIAL IN CHRONOLOGICAL SEQUENCE

In its original character as a thesis for a graduate degree,
this was the major task of the author, and since it is not quite
as readily apparent how this is done, I will give more space to
setting forth the principles by which I arrived at my chronology.
I assumed, of course, that the historical order of all the Gospels
was trustworthy *in general*. This is not an unreasonable assumption in the light of the fact that all of them give evidence

---

1. This does not in any way deny the deity of Christ but only recognizes the fact that
to his contemporaries he was a man and was addressed as a man. This writer is a devout
believer in the full deity of our Lord.

of logical progression from humble beginnings to the same climax. But to place each incident and each saying in its proper historical position is a task that has challenged the best thought of many scholars. I made a complete restudy of this whole matter and then checked my results with the results of other scholars. The wonder is not that scholars working independently have failed to come to complete agreement but that there is so much agreement among them. The results of this work in the past have been to testify to the fact that at least the main points in the chronology of the life of Christ are certain. I studied each Gospel in the light of its material, purpose, and method to determine the relative emphasis given to chronological arrangement. I assumed that each Gospel in its present form is the product of one mind which had chosen and arranged the material to fit some purpose in his own mind. I assumed also that the apparent historical form of the material is to be accepted as the true purpose unless other purposes can be adduced and proved. The results of this study were somewhat contrary to the usual opinion of scholars, but I feel that they are correct and will attempt to set forth the reasons for them in the following paragraphs. They are that Luke is to be taken as the most reliable chronological source, that John's notes of time and place are to be accepted as trustworthy, that Mark is almost always correct in this regard, but that Matthew is very questionable with respect to chronology. His material is indeed arranged in a broad historical framework, which is accurate, but the placing of specific material is more for the purpose of literary effect than for chronological accuracy. Let us notice, then, the various factors which have led to these conclusions:

Luke Made Basic in Determining Chronology

The usual conclusion has been that Mark's framework is to be adopted as basic, but I have felt that Luke is superior for the following reasons:

First, no reason can be found for the changes which Luke makes in the order of Mark except to preserve the proper historical continuity. Both Luke and Matthew make use of the Gospel of Mark as one of their main sources of material. Both of them adopt the general framework of Mark. Both of them make some changes in the specific order of Mark—Matthew far more than Luke. Matthew's changes can be traced to a desire to create the proper argumentative effect. He follows the historical order only when it suits his purpose and thinks nothing of departing from it without any other reason than to combine materials which present the argument he is seeking to establish. But this is not so with Luke. It is impossible to discover any other reason for the changes which Luke makes than the reason suggested—the desire to preserve the true chronological sequence.

This is further shown when we consider the over-all purpose of Luke in writing his Gospel. We find that purpose expressed in the beautiful preface to his Gospel: "To write to you an orderly account of them, Most Excellent Theophilus, that you might know the certainty of those things about which you have been instructed." His purpose was to write an account "in order" of the deeds and words of Jesus which would serve to prove to Theophilus the certainty of the things in which he had been given oral instruction. Much debate has centered around the meaning of the word "order" as used by Luke. Robertson says, "What kind of 'order' is it? He does not say that it is chronological order, though one naturally thinks of that."[2] If he did not mean chronological order, he meant some other kind of order, and his Gospel should show what kind it is. Matthew's Gospel shows that he is aiming at logical, argumentative order, but Luke's shows no such design.

The book is considerably longer than Mark, and shows more indications of conscious literary construction than appear in Mark. But of the influence of an argumentative aim on the structure it is impossible to discover a trace. The author seems to have aimed at an orderly account of the life of Jesus, as complete as his sources enabled him to make it without duplication of material or the use of

---

2. A. T. Robertson, *Luke the Historian in the Light of Research* (New York: Charles Scribner's Sons, 1920), p. 53.

matter which he regarded as untrustworthy . . . The only conscious purpose which we can with confidence attribute to the evangelist is that which he himself expressed in his preface, viz., on the basis of trustworthy sources and careful investigation to give an orderly and historically true narrative of the events connected with the life of Christ.[3]

This is not to say that Luke had no didactic aim. He did. He meant to teach the truth about Jesus. It is to say that he purposed to do this by letting the facts speak for themselves. No effort can successfully prove that he ever altered any account either in content or order for any other purpose than to reproduce the true historical position and content of his account.

The third reason for assigning basic value to Luke's Gospel in the matter of chronology is that, after long debate and investigation, Luke has been proved to be a historian of the first order. Leadership in this research was taken in England by Sir William Ramsay[4] and in America by Dr. A. T. Robertson[5]. In every case where it is possible to check on Luke's accuracy by secular history, unfolding evidence has proved that Luke was right all along and his critics wrong. It has been found that Luke gave a true record of the enrolment under Quirinius (Luke 2:1-5), of the beginning of Christ's ministry in the fifteenth year of Tiberius (Luke 3:1), and that his general historical trustworthiness is beyond question. A full discussion of the various problems cannot be contained in this work, but the reader is referred to the books here cited. When all the evidence is in, it will be found necessary to agree with Dr. DeMent as he says:

As an author, Luke was a historian of the first rank, who gathered material with care, sifted it with discrimination and combined it with skill. He was a man of culture and scholarly habits. He was an author of literary finish as well as one of historical accuracy.[6]

3. E. D. Burton, *A Short Introduction to the Gospels* (Chicago: The University of Chicago Press, 1908), pp. 60–62.
4. *Luke the Physician* (London: Hodder and Stoughton, Ltd., 1908) and, *Was Christ Born at Bethlehem?* (London: Hodder and Stoughton, 1898).
5. *Luke the Historian in the Light of Research.*
6. B. H. DeMent, *Bible Readers' Life of Christ* (New York: Fleming H. Revell Company, n.d.), p. 22.

I am aware of running counter to the ordinary conclusion in accepting as historically trustworthy the notes of time and place which we find in the Gospel of John. This, however, is a conclusion arrived at after a thorough study of the evidence, which changed my own opinion for the better in this regard. The reasons for this conclusion are set forth below.

The first is that they *could* be correct. It is not scholarly to decide *a priori* that they are inaccurate. Of course, it is to be admitted that they *may* be inaccurate, but their accuracy or inaccuracy will have to be established on the basis of historical evidence and not on the basis of prejudice. If John the son of Zebedee is the author of this marvelous book—and I see no reason to reject his authorship—then there is no reason to suppose that he could not have had an accurate recollection of the proper order of events. One is sometimes led to believe that the main reason for rejecting the historical accuracy of the Gospel of John is a predisposition on the part of some scholars to reject anything which smacks of the supernatural. If we are to presume that the record of the miraculous is to be thrown out of court, then, of course, we must throw John out first, for his miracles are of the most transcendent nature. But this is not historical evidence; it is theological prejudice and to the reverent scholar it has no place in court.

The next evidence, assuming that these notes of time and place could be accurate, is that the only reason which can be assigned for their presence in the record is that they were meant to be *chronological* notes. It is readily admitted that John was not writing a simple historical narrative. "His task was not the mere recording of sober history: he wished to appeal to conscience and judgment, and to refute error."[7] It has often been pointed out that John's is a spiritual Gospel. He sought to present the real Christ—the eternal Son of God. His purpose, more than that of any of the other evangelists, was to win converts, to appeal to the will and faith of the un-

---

7. H. E. Dana, *New Testament Criticism* (Fort Worth, Texas: The World Company, Inc., 1924), p. 203.

believer. But this does not necessarily mean that he made inaccurate chronological statements. Why should he? He was under no compulsion to make historical statements at all. The material which he wished to present could have been presented without making them. Yet he did make them. He, as a matter of fact, made more detailed references to time and place than did any of the other Gospel writers. Are we to assume that he was merely creating scenery for the action of his main character, that he only invented the circumstances of the incidents he records to heighten the effect?

I do not think this would be fair to the writer. We must assume that when he made a statement of time or place, he actually *thought* it was an accurate statement. It is true that the first century man was not as slavishly bound in such matters as the modern historian but he was not wholly unconscious of them. Some reason must be advanced for the compromising of his whole scheme by introducing such statements before the accuracy of the statements can be surrendered on the grounds that it was not his purpose to produce a history.

These are general statements, but they clear the way for further statements which are more specific in proving the historical accuracy of John's Gospel. The first of these is to declare that the alleged discrepancies between the Gospel of John and the Synoptics fall down of their own weight in the absence of sustaining proof. Perhaps the most serious work in this respect has been done by William Sanday (*Criticism of the Fourth Gospel*). In this book he takes up the various allegations one by one and shows them to be without foundation in fact. The most important of these have to do with the scene and duration of Christ's ministry, the cleansings of the Temple, and the date of the Last Supper.

Concerning the scene of the ministry of Christ, it is to be admitted that John presents for the most part things which took place in Judea, while the Synoptics, except for the Passion Week material, lay the scene in Galilee. But this does not mean that either is wrong. John does give room for the ministry of Jesus in Galilee and records one event—the feeding of the five thousand—in common with the Synoptics as taking place in Galilee. On the other hand, the Synoptics, though they record little which happens in Judea, are supplemented by material which John gives of the happenings in this place. And, most important of all, John does not record a single event as taking place in Judea which the Synoptics record as taking place in Galilee. While there is little contact at this point between John and the Synoptics, there is no conflict at all. If we assume that John was acquainted with the Synoptics when he wrote his Gospel, it is easy to understand why he would avoid repeating the same events which the Synoptics had already recorded.

As for the duration of the ministry of Jesus, I have the same things to say. There is no necessary conflict. None of the Gospels gives any definite statement concerning the length of the ministry of Jesus. The Synoptics do record only the one Passover feast, while John records at least three and probably four. But the Synoptic account does not state that there was *only* one; it merely records the one. It is entirely reasonable to suppose that the longer period of time which John's Passovers make necessary (either two and half or three and a half years, depending on whether the feast in 5:1 is a Passover) is itself all too short for the great movements which took place in the ministry of Jesus. It would be this writer's predisposition to accept even another year for the ministry of Jesus if there were evidence to warrant it.

There is a real discrepancy in the account of the cleansing of the Temple *if* we assume that this was done only once. But such an assumption is entirely gratuitous. There is nothing in the nature of the event which would preclude its repetition. It was such an act as any prophet might have performed. And in the eyes of the people Jesus was accepted as a prophet from the first. Further, a comparison of the records in John and Mark (John 2:13-17 and Mark 11:15-18) shows that there are differences in them which make it probable that they record two different events. In Mark there is no mention of the "scourge of small cords" nor of "sheep and oxen" in the Temple. Is it not possible that the first cleansing would have stopped this irreligious practice of bringing sheep and oxen into the Temple precincts though it did not stop the money-changers and sellers of doves? It is impossible, of course, to bring conclusive evidence to bear in either direction. But until more evidence is presented, it is the part of wisdom to accept the two accounts as such instead of trying to disparage the accuracy of either Mark or John.

The best discussion of the date of the Last Supper is to be found in Robertson's *Harmony* (pp. 281-284) in which he shows that the positive statement of the Synoptics that Jesus ate the regular Passover on the evening following the fourteenth of Nisan is not contradicted by the statements in John's Gospel. The reader is referred to a footnote on the passages involved (Sec. 153) for my conclusions in the matter.

I think it may be safely said that the various alleged discrepancies between the Synoptics and the Gospel of John are without conclusive verification and must not be accepted until proved.

We turn now to another consideration which speaks highly for the accuracy of John in matters of chronology. It is what Dr. Sanday calls the "pragmatism of the Gospel." By this term, he means the fact that the circumstances are true to the times which he presents rather than being colored by the times in which the Gospel is written. He points to the evident truth that the circumstances of Israel had greatly changed in the years between A.D. 30 and 90. The Temple was gone. The sacrifices had ceased. The Holy City was destroyed. The whole life of the nation had undergone a complete and radical change. This being true, it would be impossible for a writer unfamiliar with the events recorded to produce "an untrue narrative possessing such verisimilitude" as this Gospel does. For this Gospel is true to the circumstances of life as it was in the days of Jesus' earthly life. Dr. Sanday points out the truth of this in relation to: the pilgrimages to Jerusalem for the Jewish feasts, the detailed ceremonies connected with these feasts, the Temple itself, the state of sects and parties, and the messianic expectation.[8] Dr. Sanday uses this accumulation

---

8. William Sanday, *The Criticism of the Fourth Gospel* (New York: Charles Scribner's Sons, 1905), pp. 109-141.

of facts as an argument for the apostolic authorship of the Gospel, but it is just as cogent an argument for the historical accuracy of the writer. If John is accurate in picturing the actual conditions of the day of Jesus, why should it not be accepted that he is accurate in his statements of time and place?

These are the reasons why I have felt compelled to accept the trustworthiness of the chronological notes of John's Gospel. It may be that there is further evidence to compel another decision, but it has not come to my notice. The books which have rejected John's trustworthiness in this respect have done so without upholding (in many cases without even trying to uphold) their conclusions by evidence which is at all acceptable. Therefore, we must accept John's statements as accurate, and our chronology has been arranged in the light of this fact.

The Chronological Value of Mark

I do not mean to leave the impression that Mark is to be discarded as having no chronological value. As I have pointed out, the amazing thing is not the differences but the agreements in the Gospels. By placing Luke and John above Mark in chronological accuracy, it has been necessary in only three cases to change the order of Mark. These will be noticed by footnotes as we proceed. The noticeable thing is that Mark, seemingly without having any motive other than to present the simple facts of the wonderful Christ, has preserved a chronological framework which is unquestionable in general. I feel that the weight of evidence already pointed out is such that Mark must be placed third in the matter of chronological accuracy, but I would hasten to point out that there is virtual agreement among Mark, Luke, and John where there is parallel material.

Matthew's Chronology Questionable

When we turn to the Gospel of Matthew, we find an entirely different situation. While Matthew has built his Gospel on the general chronological framework of Mark's Gospel, there are many differences as to the placing of material, especially in the great Galilean campaign. Since it is undoubtedly true that Matthew used Mark's Gospel as one of his main sources of information, some reason for these changes must be adduced. Only two are possible: one, that he was correcting Mark's Gospel on historical grounds; the other, that he was making a rearrangement of material for argumentative effect. It is the almost unanimous opinion of New Testament scholarship that this last is true. Matthew seems to group his material for argumentative effect, bringing together those sayings or events which would prove a point. Thus the order of Matthew is logical rather than chronological. This applies also to that material which Matthew and Luke have in common (Q) where Luke seems to preserve the true historical sequence, while Matthew uses it without regard to historical setting. This does not abrogate the value of the religious message of the book, but it does place it in the lowest place so far as chronological evidence is concerned. Therefore, the material which he has in common with Mark and Luke follows their chronological position in this work. The material which is peculiar to Matthew is left in its position in Matthew's Gospel for want of evidence to force a change.

FURTHER EXPLANATIONS

The reader will notice that the Gospel material is arranged in sections which comprise incidents or discourses of Jesus. These sections are numbered consecutively throughout for the sake of easier reference. There are also larger divisions into chapters which will, it is hoped, mark the progression in the ministry of Jesus.

Technicalities have been deliberately avoided in the notes so far as possible, for two reasons: One is that the scope of the book would not permit the inclusion of sufficient material to satisfy the scholar who is interested in such matters. The other is that the audience which is anticipated for the work would not be greatly interested in them. Those who are interested in the technical study of the Gospels are referred to the abundant literature on the subject. However, it is modestly hoped that the results found in this work will show an acquaintance on the part of the author with all the problems which are involved in the study of the life of Christ.

THE AUTHOR

ACKNOWLEDGMENTS

I wish to make acknowledgment for the most important part played in the production of this book by Dr. Ray Summers professor of New Testament at Southwestern Baptist Theological Seminary in Fort Worth, Texas. It was his suggestion of the need for such a work that first started me to thinking about it as a student in the seminary. His encouragement led to the writing of a composite gospel as the thesis for my doctorate when he was my major professor. It was his encouragement also which inspired this revision into book form. Too, he has been kind enough to read the completed manuscript and offer valuable suggestions for its improvement. My only regret is that the abundance of other duties led to his refusal of my invitation to full collaboration in the production of the book.

ANALYTICAL OUTLINE

CHAPTER I

INTRODUCTION TO THE GOSPEL

CHAPTER II

BIRTH AND CHILDHOOD OF JESUS AND JOHN

CHAPTER III

THE BEGINNING OF THE MINISTRY OF JOHN

CHAPTER IV

THE BEGINNING OF JESUS' MINISTRY

CHAPTER V

CAPERNAUM ESTABLISHED AS HEADQUARTERS

CHAPTER VI

GROWING FAME AND POPULARITY IN GALILEE

CHAPTER VII

THE SABBATH CONTROVERSIES

CHAPTER VIII

CALL OF THE TWELVE AND THE SERMON ON THE MOUNT

CHAPTER IX

SPREAD OF INFLUENCE AND GROWTH OF HOSTILITY

CHAPTER X

INTENSIFIED TEACHING BY JESUS AND THE TWELVE

CHAPTER XI

SPECIAL TRAINING OF THE TWELVE

CHAPTER XII

THE LATER JUDEAN MINISTRY

CHAPTER XIII

THE LATER PEREAN MINISTRY

CHAPTER XIV

THE LAST PUBLIC MINISTRY IN JERUSALEM

CHAPTER XV

IN THE SHADOW WITH JESUS

CHAPTER XVI

A RANSOM FOR MANY

CHAPTER XVII

THE LIVING SAVIOUR

CHAPTER I

INTRODUCTION TO THE GOSPEL

Section 1. LUKE'S PREFACE

Luke 1:1-4

Since many have undertaken to arrange a detailed narrative of those things which have become fully established[1] among us just as they who were eyewitnesses and ministers of the Word from the beginning delivered them to us, it seemed good to me also, having made a thorough investigation of all things from the beginning, to write you an orderly account of them, Most Excellent Theophilus, so that you might know the certainty of those things in which you were orally instructed.[2]

Section 2. JOHN'S PROLOGUE

John 1:1-18

In the beginning the Word was, and the Word was face to face with God, and the Word was God. He was face to face with God in the beginning. All things came into being through him, and apart from him nothing came to be which came to be. In him was life, and the life was the light of men. The light keeps shining in the midst of darkness, and the darkness has not been able to extinguish it.

A man came, sent from God, whose name was John. He came as a witness, that he might bear testimony concerning the

---

1. An ambiguous term which may mean completeness either as to happening or as to knowledge of the event. I have chosen this translation purely on subjective grounds.

2. This whole passage is especially important as showing the need for the Gospels and the methods pursued in the writing of them. The need arose from the fact that new converts were orally instructed in the facts of the life of Christ. Among Gentile groups there was a need for a written record. Many had tried to meet this need by arranging a narrative of the main events in that life based on eyewitness accounts. Luke had access both to these eyewitness accounts and to the many narratives already drawn up. He had made a thorough investigation of all the matters involved and purposed to present an orderly account of them. Such language as this can only be used to describe a careful and scholarly work. It should heighten our respect for this first century historian and his fellow authors who have preserved for us the record of the marvelous life of our Lord.

[1]

light, that all men might believe through him. He was not
the light but came to bear testimony to the light.

The true light which illumines every man was coming into
the world. He was in the world, and the world came into being
through him, but the world did not know him. He came unto
his own things, and those who were his own did not receive
him. But to as many as did receive him he gave authority
to become children of God, even to those who believed on his
name. These were not begotten by blood, nor by the will of
flesh, nor by the will of man, but by God.

The Word became flesh and tabernacled among us; and we
saw his glory (glory as of the only begotten of the Father),
full of grace and truth. John testified concerning him and
cried out, This is he of whom I spoke, One comes after me who
is before me, for he was before me.

We have all received of his fulness, even grace for grace (for
the law was given through Moses, but grace and truth came
into being through Jesus Christ).

No one has seen God at any time. God's only begotten, he
who is in the bosom of the Father, he has declared him.

Section 3A. Legal Genealogy of Jesus

Matthew 1:1-17

A book of the lineage of Jesus the Messiah, son of David,
son of Abraham. Abraham was the father of Isaac. Isaac
was the father of Jacob. Jacob was the father of Judah and
his brothers. Judah was the father of Perez and Zerah by
Tamar. Perez was the father of Hezron. Hezron was the
father of Ram. Ram was the father of Aminadab. Aminadab
was the father of Nahshon. Nahshon was the father of Salmon.
Salmon was the father of Boaz by Rahab. Boaz was the father
of Obed by Ruth. Obed was the father of Jesse. Jesse was
the father of David, the king.

David was the father of Solomon by the wife of Uriah.
Solomon was the father of Rehoboam. Rehoboam was the

father of Abijah. Abijah was the father of Asa. Asa was the father of Jehoshaphat. Jehoshaphat was the father of Joram. Joram was the father of Uzziah. Uzziah was the father of Jotham. Jotham was the father of Ahaz. Ahaz was the father of Hezekiah. Hezekiah was the father of Manasseh. Mannasseh was the father of Amon. Amon was the father of Josiah. Josiah was the father of Jechoniah and his brothers at the time of the deportation to Babylon.

After the deportation to Babylon, Jechoniah became the father of Shealtiel. Shealtiel was the father of Zerrubbabel. Zerubbabel was the father of Abiud. Abiud was the father of Eliakim. Eliakim was the father of Azor. Azor was the father of Zadok. Zadok was the father of Achim. Achim was the father of Eliud. Eliud was the father of Eleazar. Eleazar was the father of Matthan. Matthan was the father of Jacob. Jacob was the father of Joseph, the husband of Mary, of whom Jesus, who is called the Messiah was born.

So all the generations from Abraham to David were fourteen; and from David to the deportation to Babylon were fourteen; and from the deportation to Babylon to the Messiah were fourteen.

Section 3B. ACTUAL GENEALOGY OF JESUS

Luke 3:23-38

Jesus was the son (as was supposed, of Joseph) of Heli,[3] the son of Matthat, the son of Levi, the son of Melchi, the son of Jannai, the son of Joseph, the son of Mattathias, the son of

---

3. These genealogies—the one recorded by Matthew and the other by Luke—have been the source of much debate among Bible scholars. The differences between the two seem to preclude the idea that they are the same table. The solution adopted above is that of Dr. A. T. Robertson, *A Harmony of the Gospels*, (Nashville, Tennessee: Baptist Sunday School Board, 1922), p. 261. To sustain the idea that Matthew gives the legal genealogy which is really the genealogy of Joseph while Luke gives the real genealogy through Mary, he gives four reasons. (1) The most natural meaning of "begat" is preserved in Matthew. Thus Jesus goes through the royal line of David and fulfills the prophecies of his coming. (2) The use of Joseph without the article in Luke's account while every other name in the list has the article. This would indicate that Joseph's name really belongs in the parenthesis with "as was supposed." Luke had already clearly stated the manner of Christ's birth so that no one would think he was the son of Joseph. (3) It would seem proper that Matthew, since he wrote primarily for the Jews, would give the legal descent. (4) Likewise, we would expect Luke, since he wrote for all, to give the real descent of Jesus. I think these reasons sufficient when coupled with the fact that no other likely explanation has been offered to establish this as the truth.

Amos, the son of Nahum, the son of Esli, the son of Naggai, the son of Maath, the son of Mattathias, the son of Semein, the son of Josech, the son of Joda, the son of Joanan, the son of Rhesa, the son of Zerubbabel, the son of Shealtiel, the son of Neri, the son of Melchi, the son of Addi, the son of Cosam, the son of Elmadam, the son of Er, the son of Jose, the son of Eliezer, the son of Jorim, the son of Matthat, the son of Levi, the son of Symeon, the son of Judas, the son of Joseph, the son of Jonam, the son of Eliakim, the son of Melea, the son of Menna, the son of Mattatha, the son of Nathan, the son of David, the son of Jesse, the son of Obed, the son of Boaz, the son of Salmon, the son of Nahshon, the son of Amminadab, the son of Arni, the son of Hezron, the son of Perez, the son of Judah, the son of Jacob, the son of Isaac, the son of Abraham, the son of Terah, the son of Nahor, the son of Serug, the son of Reu, the son of Peleg, the son of Eber, the son of Shelah, the son of Cainan, the son of Arphaxad, the son of Shem, the son of Noah, the son of Lamech, the son of Methuselah, the son of Enoch, the son of Jared, the son of Mahalaleel, the son of Cainan, the son of Enos, the son of Seth, the son of Adam, the son of God.

CHAPTER II

BIRTH AND CHILDHOOD OF JESUS AND JOHN

Section 4. ANNUNCIATION OF THE BIRTH OF JOHN

Luke 1:5-25

In the days of Herod, king of Judea, there was a priest named Zachariah of the division of Abijah who had a wife named Elisabeth, one of the daughters of Aaron. They were both upright before God, walking blamelessly in all the commandments and ordinances of God. Yet, they had no child, for Elisabeth remained barren, and they were both far advanced in age.

While he was performing his duties as priest before God when his division was on duty, he drew lot, in accordance with the custom of the priesthood, to enter the sanctuary of the Lord and burn incense. All the multitude of the people were praying outside at the hour of incense. Meanwhile there appeared to him an angel, standing at the right hand of the altar of incense. When Zachariah saw him, he was troubled and fear fell upon him.

But the angel said to him, Stop being afraid, Zachariah; your supplication has been heard, and your wife Elisabeth will bear you a son whom you shall name John. There will be great joy and exultation for you, and many will rejoice at his birth. He will be great before the Lord; he will not drink wine nor strong drink; and he will be filled with the Holy Spirit from his mother's womb. He will turn many of the sons of Israel unto the Lord their God. He will go before him in the spirit and power of Elijah to turn the hearts of fathers to their children, and the disobedient to the wisdom of the upright, to prepare for the Lord a fully equipped people.

Zachariah said to the angel, How shall I know this? I am an old man, and my wife is well advanced in age.

The angel replied, I am Gabriel who stands in the presence of God, and I was sent to speak to you and bring you this good

[5]

news.   Behold, you will be silent and unable to speak until the day when these things happen, for you have not believed my words which will be fulfilled in their time.

Meanwhile, the people were waiting for Zachariah and were wondering at his delay in the sanctuary.   When he came out, he could not speak to them.   So they knew that he had seen a vision in the sanctuary; and he kept making signs to them, but remained dumb.

When his time of service was over, he went away to his own home.   After these days, Elisabeth, his wife, conceived and hid herself for five months, saying, Thus has the Lord dealt with me in the days when he looked upon me to take away my reproach among men.

Section 5. ANNUNCIATION OF THE BIRTH OF JESUS

Luke 1:26-38

During the sixth month, the angel Gabriel was sent from God to a city of Galilee named Nazareth, to a virgin named Mary, who was betrothed to a man named Joseph, a descendant of David.

When he came to her, he said, Hail!   O favored one, the Lord is with you.

She was greatly agitated at the saying and was wondering what kind of greeting this might be.

The angel said to her, Stop being afraid, Mary.   You have found favor with God.   Lo, you will conceive and bring forth a son, and you shall name him Jesus.   He will be great and will be called the Son of the Highest, and the Lord God will give him the throne of his father David.   He will reign over the house of Jacob forever, and his kingdom will have no end.

Mary said to the angel, How can this be, since I have no husband?

The angel answered her, The Holy Spirit will come upon you, and the power of the Highest will overshadow you; wherefore, he that is born shall be called, Holy, Son of God. Lo, Elisabeth your kinswoman has also conceived a son in her old age, and this is the sixth month with her who was called barren. For no word from God is ever without power.

Mary said, Behold the bondmaid of the Lord. Let it be to me according to your word.

Then the angel left her.

Section 6. THE SONG OF ELISABETH UPON MARY'S VISIT

Luke 1:39-45

Mary arose in those days, went with haste to the hill country, to a city of Judah, came into the house of Zachariah, and greeted Elisabeth.

When Elisabeth heard the greeting of Mary, the unborn babe leaped in her womb, and Elisabeth was filled with the Holy Spirit and said with a loud shout:

Blessed are you among women,
And blessed is the fruit of your womb.
Why has it happened to me
That the mother of my Lord should come to me!

Lo, as soon as your greeting came to my ears,
The babe in my womb leaped with joy.
Blessed is she who believed,
For the Lord's promise to her will be fulfilled.

Section 7. The Magnificat of Mary

Luke 1:46-56

Then Mary said:

My soul magnifies the Lord;
My spirit rejoices in God my Saviour;
For he has looked upon the low estate of his bondmaid.
Lo, all generations will bless me from now on.

He that is mighty has done great things for me.
Holy is his name!
His mercy is unto generation after generation,
To them that fear him.

He has wrought mightily with his power;
He has scattered the proud in the purpose of their heart;
He has put down princes from their thrones and
    exalted men of low estate;
He has filled the hungry with good things and
    sent the rich away empty.

He has helped Israel, his servant,
That mercies might be remembered
As he spoke to our father,
To Abraham and to his seed forever.

Mary stayed with her about three months, then returned
to her home.

Section 8. The Birth of John and the Song of Zachariah

Luke 1:57-80

When the time was completed for Elisabeth to give birth,
she brought forth a son. Then her neighbors and relatives,
hearing that the Lord had magnified his mercy to her, rejoiced
with her.

On the eighth day, they came to circumcise the child, and they tried to call him by the name of his father, Zachariah. But his mother answered, No! He shall be called John.

They said to her, There is no one among your kindred who has this name. Then they made signs to his father to find out what he would have him called.

He asked for a small tablet and wrote, His name is John.

They were all astonished. At once his mouth was opened and his tongue loosed, and he spoke, blessing God. And fear came upon all those who lived around them. In all the hill country of Judea, these words were being talked about. All those who heard stored them up in their heart, saying, What then will this child be?

For the hand of the Lord was with him.

Zachariah, his father, was filled with the Holy Spirit, and he prophesied, saying:

Blessed is the Lord God of Israel,
For he has visited and redeemed his people.
Yes, he has raised up the horn of Salvation among us
In the house of David, his son.

Just as he spoke by the lips of his holy prophets from of old,
Salvation from our enemies and the hand of all who hate us.
To show mercy to our forefathers
And to remember his sacred covenant.

The oath which he swore to Abraham our father,
To grant us deliverance from the hand of our enemies,
So that we could serve him in holiness and righteousness
In his presence all the days of our life.

Yes, and you, child, will be called a prophet of the Highest;
You will go before the Lord to prepare his way,
To give knowledge of salvation to his people
Through the forgiveness of their sins.

Because of the tender mercies of our God,
In which the Morning Star from on High will visit us,
To shine upon those who sit in darkness, in the shadow
  of death,
To guide our feet into the way of peace.

The child grew and became strong in the Spirit, and he
was in the desert regions until the day of his public appearance
before Israel.

Section 9. JOSEPH IS REASSURED BY THE ANGEL

Matthew 1:18-25

The birth of Jesus happened like this: Mary, his mother,
having been engaged to Joseph, was found to be with child
by the Holy Spirit before they were married.   Joseph, her
husband, being an upright man and not wishing to disgrace
her publicly, resolved to put her away secretly.   But just as
he thought of this, lo, an angel of the Lord appeared to him
in a dream and said, Joseph, son of David, do not fear to take
Mary as your wife, for that which is conceived in her is of the
Holy Spirit.   She will give birth to a son, and you shall call
his name Jesus, for he will save his people from their sins.

All this happened that the word spoken by the Lord through
the prophet might be fulfilled,[1] saying:

---

1. John A. Broadus, *Commentary on the Gospel of Matthew*, Vol. I, *An American Commentary on the New Testament*, ed. Alvah Hovey (Philadelphia: The American Baptist Publication Society, 1886), p. 12.   "Some still insist that the phrase *that it might be fulfilled* should be rendered, or at any rate understood as denoting 'so that it was fulfilled,' expressing only the *result*: but the best scholars are now very nearly unanimous in maintaining that we must hold fast, in this and all similar passages, to the established meaning of the phrase.   The *design* expressed is often not merely, and in some cases not at all, that of the human agents, but the design of God in his providence.   It is probably the failure to note this simple distinction—while it was clearly perceived that in some passages no such design as that stated can have been entertained by the actors themselves—that has led numerous earlier interpreters, including some of the Greek Fathers, to accept the sense of result; and the disposition to do so has doubtless been strengthened in some minds by the dislike to the idea of divine predestination."

Lo, a virgin shall conceive and bring forth a son,
And they shall call his name Immanuel
(which, by interpretation, is, God with us).

When Joseph had awakened from his sleep, he did as the
angel of the Lord had instructed him—he received his wife.
But he did not know her until she brought forth a son. Then
he called his name Jesus.

Section 10. THE BIRTH OF JESUS

Luke 2:1-7

In those days a decree went out from Caesar Augustus to
make an enrolment of all the inhabited earth.[2] This first
took place when Quirinius was governor of Syria.

All men went to be enrolled, each to his own city. Joseph
also went up from Galilee, from the city of Nazareth, to Judea,
to the city of David which is called Bethlehem; because he
was of the house and family of David, to enroll himself and
Mary, his betrothed wife who was great with child.

While they were there, the days were completed for her
to give birth. She brought forth her first born son and wrapped

---

2. The question as to Luke's accuracy in recording this enrolment has been one of very
keen debate through many years. Dr. A. T. Robertson in *Luke the Historian in the Light of
Research* (New York: Charles Scribner's Sons, 1920), a book which takes full advantage of
earlier discoveries by Ramsay, comes to the conclusion that Luke is correct and his critics
are wrong. It is clear now that from 8 B.C. to A.D. 202 there was a periodic Roman census
taken at intervals of fourteen years. The fourteen-year cycle can be traced back to the census
of 9-8 B.C. Dr. Robertson also points out that it is entirely likely that the kingdom of Herod
would be included in the census, since the main difference between the kingdoms and the provinces in the Roman Empire was simply one of name. Too, it is pointed out that such a census
in Judea would be taken in accordance with the ancient customs of the Jews in order to mini-
mize the possibility of revolt. This would necessitate the journey of each Israelite to this
family city, hence Joseph and Mary would have come to Bethlehem. It must be admitted
that the date of 9 or even of 8 B.C. is too early for the year of the birth of Jesus. Robertson
overcomes this difficulty by supposing that some time from the issuance of the decree (which
was in 9 B.C.) would be taken up in protests and answers and organization for the census (publishing of decree, time for journeys, etc.) and it is not unlikely that the actual taking of the
census would be postponed to 5 B.C. Concerning the fact that Quirinius was governor, it is
now established that he was governor of Syria twice, though perhaps in a different sense the
first time. Certainly he was governor of Syria in 6 B.C. I think Robertson has established
his case and the record of Luke must be accepted until further evidence is produced to disprove
his accuracy.

him in swaddling clothes and laid him in a manger, for there
was no room for them in the inn.[3]

Section 11. PRAISE OF ANGELS AND HOMAGE OF SHEPHERDS
Luke 2:8-20

There were shepherds in that region who were living in the
open fields and keeping guard over their flock by night.[3]   The
angel of the Lord stood by them; the glory of the Lord shone
around them; and they were afraid with great fear.

The angel said to them, Stop being afraid; lo, I bring you
good news of great joy which shall be to all people; a saviour
who is the Lord Messiah has been born to you this day in the
city of David.

Then, suddenly, there was with the angel a multitude of
the heavenly host, praising God and saying:

Glory to God in the Highest!
Peace on earth among men of good will.

When the angels had gone away from them into heaven,
the shepherds began to say to one another, Let us go at once
to Bethlehem to see this which has come to pass, which the
Lord has made known to us.

And they went in haste and found both Mary and Joseph
and the babe lying in a manger.   When they saw him, they
told the words which were spoken to them about the child.

3. The exact date of the birth of our Lord is difficult to ascertain.   The date of the enrolment would set the limit at 8 B.C. in one direction, while the known death of Herod the great
in 4 B.C. would set the limit in that direction.   The flight to Egypt was also before the death
of Herod, and the figures of the Wise Men would make it possible that Jesus was two years old
at that time.   Thus Jesus must have been born in the four year period between 8 and 4 B.C.
The references to the fifteenth year of Tiberius in Luke 3:1-3 presents a strong presumption
in favor of the latter half of this four-year period.   Thus the most probable date was 5 or 6
B.C.   By reference to Luke 2:8, it is thought by competent scholars that the birth did not
occur in the winter at all, but during the mild months between March and November.   This
is based on the fact that during the harsh weather of the winter months, sheep were kept in
the fold at night.   No time can be decided upon with certainty.   My guess is that Jesus was
born in the early fall of 6 B.C.   This would allow for all the events recorded without unnatural
crowding.   This is only a guess, however, and a year in either direction would not impair the
Gospel narratives.

All who heard it marvelled at the words which the shepherds told them, but Mary preserved all these words and kept meditating on them in her heart.

The shepherds returned, glorifying and praising God for all that they had heard and seen even as it was spoken to them.

Section 12. THE CIRCUMCISION OF JESUS
Luke 2:21

When the eight days were fulfilled for him to be circumcised, he was named Jesus. This he was called by the angel before he was conceived in the womb.

Section 13. HOMAGE OF SIMEON AND ANNA IN THE TEMPLE
Luke 2:22-38

When the days of their purification were completed as set forth by the law of Moses, they took him up to Jerusalem to present him to the Lord (as it is written in the law of the Lord: Every male which opens the womb shall be called holy to the Lord), and to offer a sacrifice in accordance with the law of the Lord (a pair of turtle-doves or two young pigeons).

In Jerusalem, there was a just and devout man named Simeon who was waiting for the consolation of Israel, and the Holy Spirit was upon him. It had been revealed to him by the Holy Spirit that he would not see death before he had seen the Lord's Messiah. He came under the guidance of the Spirit to the temple; and when the parents brought in the child, Jesus, to do according to the custom of the law concerning him, he took him into his arms and blessed God and said:

Now, Lord, let thy slave depart
In peace, according to thy word.
For my eyes have seen thy salvation,
Which thou hast prepared in the presence of all peoples,
A light to lighten the Gentiles,
A glory to thy people, Israel.

His father and mother kept wondering at what was being said about him. Then Simeon blessed them and said to Mary his mother, Lo, he is appointed for the falling and rising again of many in Israel, and for a sign often spoken against—yes, the sword will even pierce your own soul—that the thoughts of many hearts may be revealed.

There was also a prophetess, Anna by name, a daughter of Phanuel, of the tribe of Asher. She was very old, having lived with a husband for seven years after her maidenhood, then a widow by herself until she was eighty-four years old. She never left the temple but continued to worship with fastings and prayers night and day.

At that very hour she came up and began to give thanks to God and to speak about him to all who were expecting the redemption of Jerusalem.

Section 14. The Visit of the Wise Men

Matthew 2:1-12

When Jesus was born in Bethlehem of Judea in the days of Herod the king, lo, wise men from the East came to Jerusalem, saying, Where is he that has been born King of the Jews? We saw his star in the East and have come to worship him.

King Herod, when he heard it, was troubled, and all Jerusalem with him. So he called all the chief priests and scribes of the people together and inquired of them where the Messiah was to be born. They told him, In Bethlehem of Judea, for thus it is written by the prophet:

You, Bethlehem, land of Judah,
You are surely not the least among the rulers of Judah;
For out of you shall come a governor
Who will be a shepherd of my people, Israel.

Herod secretly called the wise men and inquired carefully of them the time when the star appeared. Then he directed them to Bethlehem and said, Go and search carefully for the young child; and when you have found him, bring me tidings, that I also may come and worship him.

When they had heard the king, they went; and, lo, the star which they had seen in the East went on before them until it came and stood over the place where the young child was. When they saw the star, they rejoiced with exceedingly great joy, and coming into the house, they saw the young child with Mary, his mother. Then they fell down and worshipped him; and when they had opened their treasures, they presented unto him gifts—gold, frankincense, and myrrh.

Since they had been warned of God in a dream not to return to Herod, they retired to their own country by another route.

Section 15. THE FLIGHT TO EGYPT

Matthew 2:13-18

When they had departed, lo, the angel of the Lord appeared to Joseph in a dream, saying, Rise up, take the child and his mother, and flee into Egypt. Stay there until I tell you. Herod is going to try to destroy the Child.

So he arose and took the child and his mother and departed by night into Egypt. There he stayed until the death of Herod that the word spoken by the Lord through the prophet might be fulfilled, saying, Out of Egypt I called my Son.

When Herod saw that he had been tricked by the wise men, he was greatly enraged. He sent and killed all the male children from two years and under in Bethlehem and in all that region, according to the time which he had learned from the wise men. Then was fulfilled the word spoken through Jeremiah the prophet, saying:

> A voice was heard in Ramah,
> Weeping and great mourning,
> Rachal weeping for her children,
> And she would not be comforted,
> For they were not.

Section 16. THE RETURN TO NAZARETH

Matthew 2:19-23. Luke 2:39

As soon as Herod died, lo, the angel of the Lord appeared in a dream to Joseph in Egypt, saying, Rise up, take the child and his mother, and go into Israel. They are dead who seek the life of the child.

He arose, took the child and his mother, and came to Israel. When he heard that Archelaus was ruling over Judea instead of his father, Herod, he was afraid to go there. Having been warned of God in a dream, he went into the midst of Galilee, came and dwelt in his own city, Nazareth; in order that the word spoken through the prophet might be fulfilled, He shall be called a Nazarene.

Section 17. THE CHILDHOOD OF JESUS

Luke 2:40

The child grew and became strong, being filled with wisdom. And the favor of God was upon him.

Section 18. THE VISIT OF JESUS TO JERUSALEM AT TWELVE

Luke 2:41-50

Every year his parents went to Jerusalem for the Feast of of the Passover. When he was twelve years old, they went up in accordance with the custom of the feast. When the days were completed, they returned. But the boy Jesus remained in Jerusalem, and his parents did not know it. They supposed him to be in the caravan. After going a day's journey, they began to seek him among the kinsfolk and acquaintances. When they could not find him, they returned to Jerusalem to seek him. After three days, they found him in the temple, sitting in the midst of the teachers, hearing them and asking questions. All those who heard him were amazed at his understanding and answers. When they saw him, they were astonished; and his mother said to him, Child, why have you done this to us? Lo, your father and I have sought you in sorrow.

He replied to them, Why have you sought me? Did you not know that I must be about my Father's business?

They did not understand what he said to them.

Section 19. Eighteen Years at Nazareth

Luke 2:51-52

He returned with them to Nazareth. There, he was subject to them. His mother kept all these words carefully in her heart. And Jesus advanced in wisdom and stature, and in favor with God and man.

CHAPTER III

THE BEGINNING OF THE MINISTRY OF JOHN

Section 20. THE TIME OF THE BEGINNING

Mark 1:1. Luke 3:1-2a

The beginning of the gospel of Jesus Christ, the Son of God,[1] was in the fifteenth year of the reign of Tiberius Caesar; Pontius Pilate being governor of Judea; Herod being tetrarch of Galilee; his brother, Philip, tetrarch of Iturea and Trachonitis; and Lysanias tetrarch of Abilene; during the highpriesthood of Annas and Caiaphas.[2]

Section 21. THE MESSAGE AND THE MESSENGER

Mark 1:2-6. Matthew 3:1-6. Luke 3:2b-6

In those days, the word of God came to John, the son of Zachariah, in the wilderness. So he came preaching the baptism of repentance with reference to the remission of sins in all the desert region around the Jordan, saying, Repent, for the kingdom of heaven is at hand.

This is he of whom Isaiah the prophet spoke, saying:

> Lo, I send my messenger before you,
> Who shall prepare your way;
> A voice crying in the wilderness,
> Prepare the way of the Lord;
> Make his paths straight.

---

1. "Son of God" put in margin by Westcott Hort, but best mss. evidence (BDL) are fo ¡ts retention in text. Aleph, 28, 255 omit these words.

2. This array of chronological data should settle conclusively the question of the time when John's ministry began, but there is still some doubt. Luke tells us that Jesus was thirty years old at this time. Tiberius began to reign in A.D. 14. If we count from that time, this would be A.D. 29, which is too late even if we accept the fact that the Greek expression used by Luke means "in his early thirties." The solution is to count from A.D. 12 when Tiberius became coregent with equal authority in the provinces. This would make Jesus not more than thirty-two and would fit all the other data. Later historians did this with Titus, so Luke is correct in doing it with Tiberius.

Every valley shall be filled;
Every mountain and hill shall be levelled down;
The crooked ways shall become straight;
The rough ways shall become smooth;
And all flesh shall see the salvation of God.

John himself was clothed in camel's hair and wore a leather girdle around his loins, and his food was locusts and wild honey.

Then all the people of Jerusalem and all Judea and all the country around the Jordan began to go out to him and were being baptized by him in the Jordan River, confessing their sins.

Section 22. Specimen of John's Preaching

Matthew 3:7-10. Luke 3:7-14

When he saw many of the Pharisees and Sadducees among the crowds that came out to be baptized by him, he said to them, You brood of vipers, who has warned you to flee from the coming wrath? Produce fruits worthy of repentance; and think not within yourselves to say, We have Abraham as a father, for I say unto you that God is able to raise up children to Abraham from these stones. Already the axe is laid to the root of the trees; every tree therefore which does not produce good fruit is cut down and cast into the fire.

The multitude asked him, saying, What then shall we do?

He answered them, Let him that has two coats share with him who has none, and let him who has food do likewise.

Even the tax collectors came to him to be baptized and said, Teacher, what shall we do?

He answered them, Stop exacting more than the prescribed rate.

So also did the soldiers ask him, And, we, what shall we do?

He answered them, Intimidate no man. Accuse no one falsely. Be content with your wages.

Section 23. John's Description of the Messiah

Mark 1:7-8.   Matthew 3:11-12.   Luke 3:15-18

The people became tense with expectancy. They were debating in their hearts concerning John, whether he might be the Messiah.

John answered them all, I indeed baptize you in water with reference to repentance. But another and greater one comes after me, whose sandals I am not worthy to untie; he will baptize you in the Holy Spirit and fire. His winnowing fork is in his hand to clean up his threshing floor and to gather the wheat into his granary; but the straw he will burn in unquenchable fire.

So, with many other exhortations, John continued to preach the gospel to the people.

CHAPTER IV

THE BEGINNING OF JESUS' MINISTRY

Section 24. THE BAPTISM OF JESUS

Mark 1:9-11.   Matthew 3:13-17.   Luke 3:21-23

Now in those same days, while all the people were being baptized, Jesus also came from Nazareth of Galilee to be baptized by John in the Jordan.   But John tried to prevent him, saying, I have need to be baptized by you; and do you come to me?

Jesus answered him, Let it be so now, for this is the way for us to complete all righteousness.

So he permitted him.

When Jesus had been baptized, he came up out of the water, praying.   And, lo, the heavens were opened and he saw the Holy Spirit of God descending upon him in physical form as a dove.   Behold, a voice came out of the heavens saying, You are my Beloved Son; I am well pleased with you.

Section 25. THE TEMPTATION OF JESUS

Mark 1:12-13.   Matthew 4:1-11.   Luke 4:1-13

Then Jesus, full of the Holy Spirit, returned from the Jordan; he was led by the Spirit into the wilderness to be tempted forty days by the devil; and he lived with the wild beasts.   During those forty days and forty nights he ate nothing, so when they were completed, he was hungry.   The devil came to him and said, Since you are the Son of God, tell these stones to become bread.

Jesus replied, It is written, Man does not live by bread alone but by every word that comes from the mouth of God.

[21]

Then the devil took him into the Holy City, Jerusalem, and placed him upon the parapet of the temple and said to him, Since you are the Son of God, throw yourself down from here. For it is written, He will give command to his angels concerning you to guard you carefully, and, On their hands they will bear you up lest you strike your foot against a stone at any time.

Jesus answered him, Again it is written, You shall not tempt the Lord your God.

Again, the devil took him up to a very high mountain and showed him all the kingdoms of the world and their glory in an instant. Then the devil said to him, I am willing to give you all this authority and their glory, for it has been given to me and I give it to whom I desire; if you will fall down and worship before me, it will be yours.

Jesus answered him, Get behind me, Satan; for it is written, You shall worship the Lord your God and him only shall you serve.[1]

The devil, having completed every temptation, departed from him for a season.

And, lo, the angels came and ministered to him.

Section 26. JOHN DENIES THAT HE IS THE MESSIAH

John 1:19-28

Now this is what John said when the Jews of Jerusalem sent priests and Levites to ask him, Who are you?

He confessed—he did not deny it, but freely confessed—I am not the Messiah.

They asked him, What then? Are you Elijah?

He said, I am not.

---

1. Matthew's order of temptations has been followed because it seems the more logical

Are you the Prophet?

He answered, No.

They said to him, Who are you? We must give some answer to them who sent us. What have you to say about yourself?

He said, I am the voice of one crying in the wilderness, Make straight the way of the Lord; just as Isaiah the prophet said.

They had been sent by the Pharisees. So they asked him, Why then are you baptizing if you are not the Messiah nor Elijah nor the Prophet?

John answered them, I am baptizing in water; another is standing among you whom you do not know, he who comes after me, but whose sandals I am not worthy to unfasten.

These things happened in Bethany beyond Jordan where John was baptizing.

Section 27. JOHN IDENTIFIES THE MESSIAH

John 1:29-34

The next day, he saw Jesus coming toward him and said, Behold the Lamb of God who takes away the sins of the world. This is he of whom I said, A man comes after me who has been placed before me, because he was before me. I did not know him myself, but I had come baptizing in water so that he might be revealed to Israel.

John also testified, I saw the Spirit descending as a dove out of heaven and it continued to rest upon him. I would not have recognized him myself; but he who sent me to baptize in water said to me, Upon whomever you see the Spirit descending and abiding, he is the one who baptizes in the Holy Spirit. I have seen it and do testify that this is the Son of God.

Section 28. Jesus Makes His First Disciples
John 1:35-51

Again the next day, John was standing with two of his disciples, and when he saw Jesus walking by, he said, Lo! See! there is the Lamb of God.

The two disciples heard him speak and followed Jesus.

Jesus turned around and saw them following him. He said to them, What are you seeking?

They answered him, Rabbi (which means, Teacher), where do you live?

He said to them, Come and see.

Therefore they came and saw where he lived, and they stayed with him that day. It was about ten in the morning .

Andrew, the brother of Simon Peter, was one of the two disciples who heard John and followed him. The first thing he did was to find Simon, his own brother, and say to him, We have found the Messiah (which means, the Christ). He brought him to Jesus.

When Jesus saw him, he said, You are Simon, the son of John. You shall be called Cephas (which means, Rock[2]).

The next day he wished to go to Galilee, and he found Philip. Jesus said to him, Follow me.

Philip was from Bethsaida, the city of Andrew and Peter. Philip found Nathanael and said to him, We have found him of whom Moses, in the law, and the prophets wrote, Jesus the son of Joseph of Nazareth.

Nathanael said to him, Is it possible for any good thing to come from Nazareth?

Philip said, Come and see.

---

2. In the older translations the Greek word is transliterated to "Peter," but its correct translation is "rock."

Jesus saw Nathanael coming to him and said of him, See! here is a true Israelite, one in whom there is no guile.

Nathanael said to him, Where did you learn of me?

Jesus answered him, Before Philip called you, while you were under the fig tree, I saw you.

Nathanael answered him, Rabbi, you are the Son of God. You are the king of Israel.

Jesus answered him, Do you believe because I told you that I saw you under the fig tree? You will surely see greater things than this.

Then he said to him, Truly, truly, I say to you, you will see heaven opened, and the angels of God ascending and descending ~~upon the~~ Son of man.

To THE (enter)

Section 29. JESUS PERFORMS HIS FIRST MIRACLE

John 2:1-11

Two days later there was a wedding in Cana of Galilee, and the mother of Jesus was a guest. Jesus also was invited with his disciples to the wedding. When the wine gave out, the mother of Jesus said to him, They have no wine.

Jesus said to her, What have we in common, woman?[3] My hour is not yet come.

His mother instructed the servants, Do what he tells you.

There were six waterpots of stone placed there in accordance with the purification ceremonies of the Jews. Each one held twenty or thirty gallons. Jesus said to them, Fill the pots with water.

They filled them up to the brim.

Then he told them, Draw out now and serve the ruler of the feast.

---

3. Greek idiom which suggests that they were looking at the situation from differing standpoints.

They carried it to him.

When the ruler of the feast tasted the water which had become wine, he did not know where it came from, but the servants who had drawn out the water knew. The ruler of the feast called the bridegroom and said to him, Every man usually serves good wine at first, and when the guests have become intoxicated, the inferior. But you have kept the good wine until now.

This—the beginning of signs—Jesus did in Cana of Galilee His glory was revealed, and his disciples believed on him

Section 30. A TEMPORARY VISIT TO CAPERNAUM

John 2:12

After this, he went down to Capernaum with his mother, his brothers, and his disciples. They stayed there only a few days.

Section 31. JESUS CLEANSES THE TEMPLE

John 2:13-22

The Passover of the Jews was near, so Jesus went up to Jerusalem. There he found those in the temple who were selling oxen, sheep, and pigeons, and the money-changers sitting at their tables. Making a whip of cords he drove them all out, both the sheep and the oxen. Then he poured out the money of the money-changers and overturned the tables; and to those who sold the doves he said, Take these things out. Stop making my Father's house a market place.[4]

---

4. John records this as taking place in the beginning of the ministry of Jesus. Mark records the same event or a similar one during the passion week. A discrepancy exists in chronology—not in message—if they are the same. But it is not necessary to assume that they are. This was an act which any prophet might have performed and Jesus was certainly accepted as a prophet from the beginning. It had no necessary messianic implications. Witness the reaction of the Pharisees. Too, it was an act which would need periodic repetition. This illegitimate trafficking in the Temple was so lucrative that it would be hard to put a permanent stop to it. Notice, too, that differences in the two narratives is such that similar, rather than the same, events are indicated. In Mark there is no mention of the "whip of small cords" nor of "sheep and oxen" in the Temple. Is it not possible that the first cleansing would have corrected this irreligious practice of bringing sheep and oxen into the Temple precincts, though it did not stop the money-changers and the sellers of doves? Until more evidence is available, we must accept the twofold cleansing as correct.

His disciples remembered that it is written, Zeal for your house will consume me.

Then the Jews said to Jesus, What sign do you show us, that you have a right to do these things?

Jesus answered them, Destroy this temple, and I will raise it up in three days.

The Jews said, It has taken forty-six years to build this temple and will you raise it in three days?

But he was speaking of the temple of his body. When he was raised from the dead, his disciples remembered that he said this, and they believed the Scripture and the word of Jesus.

Section 32. JESUS' INTERVIEW WITH NICODEMUS

John 2:23 to 3:21

While he was in Jerusalem for the Passover, many believed in his name during the feast because they saw the signs which he did. But Jesus did not trust himself to them because he knew all men. He had no need for anyone to tell him about man, for he himself knew what was in man.

There was a man of the Pharisees named Nicodemus, a ruler of the Jews. He came to him one night and said, Rabbi, we know that you are a teacher come from God, for no one is able to do these signs which you are doing unless God is with him.

Jesus answered him, Truly, truly, I tell you, except a man be born again, he cannot see the kingdom of God.

Nicodemus said to him, How is it possible for a man to be born when he is old? He could not enter a second time into his mother's womb and be born, could he?

Jesus replied, Truly, truly, I say to you, except a man be born of water and Spirit, he cannot enter the kingdom of God.

What is born of the flesh is flesh, but what is born of the Spirit
is spirit. Do not marvel that I told you, You must be born
again. The wind blows where it wishes. You hear its sound,
but you do not know where it comes from nor where it goes.
So is every one who is born of the Spirit.

Nicodemus answered him, How can these things be?

Jesus said to him, Are you a teacher of Israel without knowing these things? Truly, truly, I say to you, we know what
we speak and have seen what we tell you of, but you will not
receive our testimony. If I have told you earthly things and
you do not believe, how can you believe if I tell you heavenly
things.

Now no one has ascended into heaven except the Son of
man who came down from heaven. Just as Moses lifted up
the serpent in the wilderness, the Son of man must be lifted up,
in order that whoever believes in him may have eternal life.
For God so loved the world that he gave his only begotten Son
that whoever believes in him should not perish but have eternal
life. God did not send his Son into the world that he might
condemn the world, but that the world might be saved through
him. He who believes in him is not condemned; but he who
does not believe is already condemned, because he has not
believed in the name of the only begotten Son of God. This
is the condemnation: light has come into the world, and men
loved darkness rather than light because their deeds were evil.
For every one who practices evil hates the light and will not
come to the light, lest his works should be exposed. But he
that practices truth comes to the light that his works might
be proved to be wrought in God.

Section 33. JOHN'S LOYALTY TESTED

John 3:22-36

After this, Jesus and his disciples came into the land of
Judea. There he tarried with them and was baptizing. John
also was baptizing at Enon near Salem because there was much

water there, and men continued to come and be baptized.
For John had not yet been put in prison. There arose a discussion between the disciples of John and a Jew concerning
purification. So they came to John and said to him, Rabbi, lo,
he who companied with you beyond the Jordan, to whom you
gave testimony, is baptizing, and all men are coming to him.

John replied, Man can receive nothing but what is given
him from heaven. Even you bear me witness that I said, I am
not the Messiah, but am sent before him. He who has the
bride is the bridegroom, but the friend of the bridegroom who
stands and hears him is filled with joy because of the voice of
the bridegroom. This, my joy, has therefore been fulfilled.
He must increase, but I must decrease.

He that comes from above is above all; he who is of the
earth is of the earth and speaks of the earth. He who is from
heaven is above all. He tells what he has seen and heard,
but no man receives his testimony. He who receives his testimony has set his seal on this, that God is true. He whom God
sent speaks the word of God, for the Spirit is given to him
without limitation. The Father loves the Son and has put
all things into his hands. He who believes in the Son has
eternal life; he who refuses to obey the Son shall not see life,
but the wrath of God continues to abide on him.

Section 34. JESUS' REASONS FOR LEAVING JUDEA

Mark 1:14.   Matthew 4:12.   Luke 3:19-20; 4:14a.   John 4:1-4

Herod, the tetrarch, being repeatedly reproved by him
(John) concerning Herodias the wife of his brother and all the
evil things which Herod had done, added this sin to all the rest:
he shut John up in prison.

When the Lord heard that John was delivered—since he
knew that the Pharisees had heard that he was making and
baptizing more disciples than John (though Jesus himself was

not baptizing but his disciples)—he left Judea and returned in the power of the Spirit to Galilee. He had to go through Samaria.

Section 35. JESUS IN SAMARIA

John 4:5-42

Therefore he came to a city of Samaria called Sychar, near the estate which Jacob gave to his son Joseph. Jacob's well was there. Because he was tired from the journey, Jesus sat thus on the well; it was about six in the afternoon. A woman of Samaria came to draw water. Jesus said to her, Give me a drink (for his disciples had gone into the city to buy food).

The Samaritan woman said to him, How is it that you being a Jew ask me, a woman of the Samaritans, for a drink? (For the Jews had nothing to do with the Samaritans.)

Jesus answered her, If you knew the gift of God and who it is that says to you, Give me a drink, you would have asked him, and he would have given you living water.

She said to him, Sir, you have no vessel to draw with and the well is deep. Where then can you obtain living water? You are not greater than our father Jacob who gave us this well and drank of it himself and his sons and his cattle, are you?

Jesus answered her, Every one who drinks of this water will thirst again, but whoever drinks of the water which I give him shall never thirst. The water which I give him shall be in him a spring of water springing up to eternal life.

The woman said, Sir, give me this water that I may never thirst, neither come here to draw water.

He said to her, Go call your husband and come here.

The woman answered, I have no husband.

Jesus said to her, You speak the truth when you say, I have no husband, for you have had five husbands, and the one you have now is not your husband. Thus you told the truth.

The woman said, Sir, I see that you are a prophet. Our forefathers worshipped in this mountain, but you say that Jerusalem is the place where men must worship.

Jesus said to her, Believe me, woman, the hour is coming when you will not worship the Father in this mountain nor in Jerusalem. You do not know what you worship; we know what we worship, for salvation is of the Jews. But the hour is coming and now is when true worshippers will worship the Father in spirit and truth, for the Father seeks such to worship him. God is Spirit. Those who worship him must worship in spirit and truth.

The woman said, I know that the Messiah is coming (he who is called Christ), when he comes, he will tell us all things.

Jesus said to her, I who speak to you am he.

Just then his disciples returned, and they were marveling that he was speaking to a woman. However, no one said, What do you seek, or, Why do you speak to her.

The woman left her waterpot and went into the city. There she said to the men, Come and see a man who told me everything that I ever did. This is not the Messiah, is it?

They left the city and were making their way to him.

Meanwhile the disciples asked him, saying, Rabbi, eat.

He said to them, I have food to eat of which you know nothing.

The disciples began to say to one another, Has anyone brought him food?

Jesus replied, My food is to do the will of him who sent me and to complete his work. Do you not say that it is yet four months to the harvest? Lo, I tell you, lift up your eyes and see the fields, for they are white for the harvest. Already the reaper is receiving wages and gathering fruit unto eternal life. Thus, he that sows and he that reaps will both rejoice together; for this is a true word: One sows and another reaps. I have sent you to reap where you have not labored. Others labored and you have entered into their labor.

Many of the Samaritans of that city believed in him because of the word of the woman who testified, He told me all that I ever did. So when the Samaritans came to him, they asked him to stay with them. He stayed there two days. Many more believed because of his word and were saying to the woman, We no longer believe because of your testimony, for we also have heard, and we know that this is truly the Saviour of the world.

CHAPTER V

CAPERNAUM ESTABLISHED AS HEADQUARTERS

Section 36. Jesus Begins His Ministry in Galilee

Mark 1:14-15.   Matthew 4:17.   Luke 4:14-15.   John 4:43,45

After two days he left there and came into Galilee preaching the gospel of God and saying, The time has been fulfilled.   The kingdom of God has come near.   Repent and believe the gospel.[1]

His fame spread throughout all the surrounding country, and the Galileans received him because they had seen all the things that he did in Jerusalem at the feast; for they also had gone to the feast.   He began to teach in their synagogues and was being praised by all men.

Section 37. The Son of a Nobleman Healed

John 4:46-54

He came, therefore, again to Cana of Galilee where he had made the water become wine.   There was a certain official whose son was sick at Capernaum.   When he heard that Jesus had come out of Judea into Galilee, he came to him and asked him to come down and heal his son; for he was about to die.

Jesus said to him, You will not believe unless you see signs and wonders.

The official said to him, Lord, come down before my son dies.

Jesus said to him, Go.   Your son lives.

He believed the word which Jesus said to him, and the man started back at once.   While he was on the way, his slaves met him and began to tell him that his son was living.   Then he inquired of them the hour when he began to mend.

---

1. John does not record either of the visits to the city of Nazareth.   He inserts here the saying of Jesus concerning the prophet's honor in his own country.   The Synoptics record this on the occasion of the visits to Nazareth, and their order has been followed.

They said to him, Yesterday at seven the fever left him.

Then the father knew that it was at the same hour when Jesus had said to him, Your son lives.

He and his whole house believed.

This again was the second sign which Jesus did when he came out of Judea into Galilee.

Section 38. JESUS REJECTED AT NAZARETH

Luke 4:16-30

He came to Nazareth[2] where he had been brought up and attended the synagogue on the sabbath as his custom was. There he stood up to read, and the roll of the prophet Isaiah was given to him; when he opened the roll, he found the place where it is written:

The Spirit of the Lord is upon me,
Because he has anointed me to preach good news to the poor.
He has sent me to preach deliverance to captives,
And recovery of sight to the blind;
To set free men who are oppressed;
To proclaim the acceptable year of the Lord.

He closed the roll and gave it back to the attendant and sat down. The eyes of all who were in the synagogue were fixed on him. He began to say to them, Today this scripture has been fulfilled in your hearing.

---

2. The question arises, Is the same visit recorded by both Luke and Mark, or did Jesus make two visits to his home town? Not much is at stake in either case. However, the evidence seems to point to two visits. There is no reason why two visits could not be made. But there is every reason to believe that the Lord would make more than one effort to reach the hearts of his own townspeople. Too, the records are divergent enough that more problems are raised by making them refer to the same occasion than by taking them as records of different visits. In Luke, the address of Jesus engenders wrath that ends in an attempt to kill him. There is no room for this in Matthew and Mark. In Luke's visit the people expect him to work miracles, and he refuses to do so. Mark and Matthew picture him as anxious to work them but unable to because of the unbelief of the people. Of course it is impossible to be dogmatic, but until further evidence is uncovered, it seems that the weight of evidence is in favor of the two-visit hypothesis.

They all began to testify of him and to marvel at the gracious words which came from his mouth, and they kept saying, This one is the son of Joseph, is he not?

He answered them, You will surely quote this proverb to me: Physician, heal yourself; do here in your native place all that we have heard that you did in Capernaum.

He continued, Truly, I say to you, No prophet is acceptable in his native place. I tell you of a truth, there were many widows in Israel in the days of Elijah when the heavens were shut up for three years and six months and great famine came to the land; to none of them was Elijah sent, but to a widow of Zarephath in the land of Sidon. Too, there were many lepers in Israel in the time of Elisha the prophet; not one of them was cleansed save only Naaman, the Syrian.

When they heard these things, the men in the synagogue were all filled with wrath. They rose up and cast him out of the city and led him to a cliff on the hill on which their city was built to throw him down headlong. But he passed through the midst of them and went away.

Section 39. JESUS ESTABLISHES HEADQUARTERS AT CAPERNAUM

Matthew 4:13-16. Luke 4:31a

So he left Nazareth and came to Capernaum to live, a city of Galilee which is beside the sea in the region of Zebulun and Naphtali. This was to fulfill the word spoken through Isaiah, the prophet:

Land of Zebulun and land of Naphtali,
On the way to the sea across Jordan,
Galilee of the Gentiles,
The people who sat in darkness
Have seen a great light,
And those who sat in the region and shadow of death,
Upon them has the light risen.

CHAPTER VI

GROWING FAME AND POPULARITY IN GALILEE

Section 40. The Four Invited to Accompany Jesus

Mark 1:16-20.   Matthew 4:18-22

As he was walking beside the Sea of Galilee, he saw two brothers—Simon who is called Peter, and Andrew, his brother —casting a net into the sea, for they were fishermen. Jesus said to them, Follow me: I will make you to become fishers of of men.[1]

They immediately left their nets and followed him.

And going a little farther along, he saw two other brothers— James the son of Zebedee, and John, his brother—in the boat with Zebedee their father, mending their nets. Them he called also. They, too, leaving their father Zebedee in the boat with the hired servants, followed him at once.

Section 41. Jesus Heals a Demoniac

Mark 1:21-28. Luke 4:31b-37

He came into Capernaum and on the first sabbath went into the synagogue and began to teach. They were completely astonished at his teachings, for he was teaching like one who had authority and not like the scribes. There was in the synagogue a man with an unclean spirit who cried out with a

---

1. Luke records a similar story after the first tour of Galilee. Is it the same as this story and misplaced, or did this take place twice? This depends on our view of what is involved in this call. John's Gospel has already given us cause to know that these men were already believers in Jesus—at least Andrew and Peter were. This was not a call to belief. Nor was it a call to apostleship and constant companying with him. This came later on. It seems to have been simply an invitation to go with him on this tour of the cities of Galilee. If so, it is reasonable to suppose that when the tour is finished, they will return to their occupation. Later, it became necessary to make another tour and they were invited again. This is the call Luke records. This view is upheld by two considerations. One, Luke is usually accurate in his placing of material. Two, the differences in the two accounts seems to preclude the idea that they are records of the same experience. In Luke we have the pressing crowd, the miraculous catch of fishes, and the consternation of Peter. There is no room for any of this in this account.

loud voice, Ho! what do you want with us, Jesus of Nazareth? Have you come to destroy us? I know who you are—the the Holy One of God.

Jesus rebuked him, saying, Be still and come out of him.

After the demon threw him down in their midst and cried out with a loud voice, he came out of him without doing him any harm.

They were all so amazed that they discussed it with one another, saying, What word is this? a new teaching? with authority and power he commands even the unclean spirits, and they obey him and come out.

And the report concerning him went out to every place in the whole surrounding region of Galilee.

Section 42. The Healing of Peter's Mother-in-law

Mark 1:29-34.   Matthew 8:14-17.   Luke 4:38-41

He arose and left the synagogue at once and entered the house of Simon Peter with Andrew, James, and John. Simon's mother-in-law lay prostrate with a great fever. They told him at once and besought him for her. As soon as he came up to her and rebuked it, the fever left her. Then he took her by the hand and lifted her up and she began to serve them.

When evening came, even while the sun was setting, they began to bring those who were ill with various diseases and those who were demon-possessed to him. The whole city was assembled at the door. He laid his hands upon each one of them and healed many who were diseased with various infirmities. He cast out many evil spirits with a word; and when they came out, they cried and said, You are the Son of God.

But he rebuked them and would not let them speak, because they knew that he was the Messiah.

This was a fulfillment of the word spoken by Isaiah the prophet:

He himself took away our infirmities
And bore our diseases.

Section 43. A PREACHING TOUR OF GALILEE

Mark 1:35-39.   Matthew 4:23-25.   Luke 4:42-44

Long before daybreak the next morning, he arose, went out to a desert place, and prayed there.   But the crowds were continuing to seek him.

Simon and those who were with him sought him out; and when they found him, they said, All men are seeking you.

The multitudes who sought him also came up and would have stopped his departure from them.   But he said to them, I must preach the good news of the kingdom of God in other cities also.

To the disciples he said, Let us go on into the next towns that I may preach there, for I came out here for this cause.

So he went throughout all Galilee teaching in their synagogues, preaching the good news of the kingdom, casting out demons, and healing all diseases and all kinds of sickness among the people.

The report about him went out to all Syria; and they began to bring to him all who were ill, having various kinds of diseases and pains—demoniacs, epileptics, and paralytics; and he healed them.   Then great multitudes followed him from Galilee, Decapolis, Jerusalem, Judea, and beyond Jordan.

Section 44. ANOTHER INVITATION TO COMPANY WITH JESUS

Luke 5:1-11

Once while the crowd was pressing upon him and listening to the word of God, he himself was standing on the shore of the Lake of Gennesaret.   He saw two boats moored by the shore, but the fishermen were gone out of them, washing their nets. He got into one of the boats, which belonged to Simon, and asked him to put out a short distance from the shore. Then he sat down and continued to teach the crowds from the boat.

When he stopped talking, he said to Simon, Put out into the deep and let down your nets for a catch.

Simon replied, Master, we have been toiling all night and have caught nothing. Nevertheless, at your word, I will let down the nets.

This they did and caught so many fish that their nets began to break. They signaled for their partners to come and help them with the other boat. When they came, they filled both boats so full that they began to sink.

When Simon Peter saw this, he fell down at the knees of Jesus and said, Depart from me, Lord, for I am a sinful man.

For bewilderment had seized him and all those with him at the catch of fishes which they had made, and likewise also James and John, the Sons of Zebedee, who were partners with Simon.

Jesus said to Simon, Stop being afraid. From now on you will catch men alive.

They brought the boats to land, left everything, and followed him.

Section 45. THE HEALING OF A LEPER

Mark 1:40-45. Matthew 8:2-4. Luke 5:12-16

Lo, there was a man full of leprosy in one of the cities where he went. When he saw Jesus, he came to him, fell down, and worshipped him, saying, Lord, if you are willing, you can make me clean.

He was filled with pity and stretched out his hand and touched him, saying, I am willing. Be clean.

The leprosy left him at once and he was clean.

He sternly admonished him and sent him away, saying, See that you tell this to no man, but go show yourself to the priest and offer with reference to your cleansing the gifts which Moses commanded for a witness to them.

But he went out and began to proclaim it much and to spread abroad the word, so that his fame spread the more. And such great crowds came together to hear and to be healed of their infirmities that he was no longer able to go publicly into a city, but continued his practice of retiring to lonely places and praying. But they continued to come to him from every direction.

Section 46. A Paralytic Is Healed

Mark 2:1-12. Matthew 9:1-8. Luke 5:17-26

Afterward, he entered into his own city, Capernaum. One day while he was there, he began to teach. There were Pharisees and doctors of law who had come out of all the villages of Galilee and Judea and Jerusalem sitting around. When it became known that he was at home, so many gathered together that there was no room left, not even at the door. He kept speaking the word to them, and the power of the Lord was upon him to heal.

And, lo, four men came, bringing a paralytic man to him, prostrated on his pallet, seeking to enter and lay him before him. They could not come near him because of the crowd, so they went up on the roof and dug through the roofing over his head. Then they lowered the pallet on which the paralytic lay into the midst of the crowd before Jesus. When Jesus saw their faith, he said to the paralytic, Take courage, son, your sins are forgiven.

Some of the scribes and Pharisees began to reason in their hearts, saying, who is this one that he should speak so? It is blasphemy. Who is able to forgive sins except God only?

Jesus perceived at once in his spirit that they reasoned so, and answered them, Why do you imagine evil things in your hearts? Which is easier: to say, Your sins are forgiven, or to say, Arise, take up your pallet, and walk? But that you may know that the Son of Man has authority on earth to forgive sins . . . .

He said to the paralytic, I say to you, arise, take up your pallet, and go to your own house.

Immediately, he arose before them all, took up his pallet, and went to his house, glorifying God.

The crowd was afraid, and astonishment laid hold on all of them, so that they glorified God who had given such authority to men, saying, We have seen a paradox today such as we never saw before.

Section 47. THE CALL AND FEAST OF LEVI

Mark 2:13-17. Matthew 9:9-13. Luke 5:27-32

He went out again by the side of the sea, and all the crowd came to him, and he continued to teach them. As Jesus passed on, he saw Levi (who is also called Matthew), the son of Alphaeus, sitting at the place where taxes were paid; and he said to him, Follow me.

He rose up, forsook all, and followed him. Now Levi made a great feast for him in his house. As he reclined at dinner, a great crowd of tax-collectors and sinners reclined with him and his disciples, for many were his followers.

The Pharisees and scribes, seeing that he ate with tax collectors and sinners, began to grumble and to say to his disciples, Why do you and your teacher eat with tax-collectors and sinners?

But Jesus heard them and answered, They who are well have no need for a physician, but they who are sick. Go learn what this means: I will have mercy and not sacrifice. I have not come to call the righteous but sinners to repentance.

Section 48. Jesus Answers Questions About Fasting

Mark 2:18-22.   Matthew 9:14-17.   Luke 5:33-39

The disciples of John and the Pharisees were in the habit of fasting. So they came to him and said, The disciples of John fast often and make supplication; likewise also they of the Pharisees; but your disciples never fast, but eat and drink. Why is this?

Jesus answered them, You cannot make the wedding guests fast and mourn while the bridegroom is with them. As long as the bridegroom is with them, they cannot fast. But days are coming when the bridegroom will be taken from them; they will fast in those days.

He spoke also a parable to them. No man sews a patch of unshrunk material on an old garment. If he does, the new that is meant to mend tears away the old and a worse tear is made. Certainly no one tears a patch from a new garment to sew it on an old one; if he does, he will tear the new one also and the patch from it will not match the old one.

Neither does a man put new wine into old wine skins. If he does, the new wine will burst the skin and the wine will pour out, and the old skin will perish as well. He puts the new wine in a new skin and both are kept safe. Nor does one who has drunk old wine call for new. He says, The old is good enough.

CHAPTER VII

THE SABBATH CONTROVERSIES

Section 49. A LAME MAN HEALED ON THE SABBATH

John 5:1-47

After these things there was a feast[1] of the Jews and Jesus went up to Jerusalem. In Jerusalem there is a pool near the sheep gate which is called in Hebrew, Bethzatha, which has five porches. In these lay a multitude of sick, blind, crippled, and paralyzed.[2] Among them was a man who had had an infirmity for thirty eight years.

When Jesus saw this one lying there, knowing that he had had it for a long time already, he said to him, Would you like to become whole?

The sick man answered, Sir, I have no one to put me in the pool when the water is troubled. While I am coming, another gets down before me.

Jesus said to him, Arise, take up your pallet and walk

Immediately the man became whole and took up his pallet and walked. Now this was on the sabbath day.

---

1. Was this feast a passover of the Jews? On the answer to this question will depend the length of the ministry of Jesus. No great doctrinal problem, however, is involved, nor one of chronology. The scholars differ on this point, but stronger probability is in favor of this being a passover. Dr. Robertson, in his *Harmony*, gives the following arguments in favor of this view: (a) The plucking of ears from standing grain by the disciples would indicate a time after the Passover and before Pentecost (Luke 6:1). (b) It is fairly implied (John 5:1) that the feast took Jesus to Jerusalem. The Passover would be more likely to be the one to lead him there. (c) This suits best the hostility manifested at this feast, which would have time to become acute and break out with increased vigor in Galilee and prevent his attending the next Passover (John 6:4; 7:1). (d) If this Passover be a second Passover of the ministry, sufficient time is afforded for the great Galilean ministry without artificial crowding. Only two serious objections can be urged. (1) The absence of the article indicates some other feast. But the article is included in some texts. However, its absence is not conclusive because this word is used without the article to mean the Passover (Matt. 27:15; Mark 15:6). (2) The chief objection is that a year and six months is too long for Jesus to have stayed away from Jerusalem. But we do not know that he did not attend some other feast which is not recorded. If he did stay away, the hostility of the Jews is sufficient explanation of his reason.

2. Many ancient authorities insert: waiting for the moving of the water. For an angel came down at certain times into the pool, and troubled the water. He therefore who first entered after the troubling of the water was made whole of whatever disease he was held.

The Jews therefore said to him who was healed, This is the sabbath and it is not lawful for you to carry your pallet.

He answered them, The man who made me whole said to me, Take up your pallet and walk.

They asked him, Who is the man who told you to take it up and walk?

But he who was healed did not know who he was, for Jesus had withdrawn, a multitude being in that place.

Afterward, Jesus found him in the temple and said to him, See, you are whole. Live no longer in sin lest a worse thing happen to you.

The man went to the Jews and told them that Jesus was the man who had made him whole. Therefore the Jews began to persecute Jesus because he did this on the sabbath.

He began to answer them, My Father is working up till now, and I am working.

For this reason, the Jews sought the more to kill him, not only because he broke the sabbath but also because he claimed that God was his own Father, thus making himself equal with God.

But Jesus kept talking to them, Truly, truly, I tell you, the Son is able to do nothing by himself, but only what he sees the Father doing. Whatever he does, the Son likewise does. The Father loves the Son and shows him all the things which he himself does, and greater works than these will he show him that you may marvel. For as the Father raises the dead and gives them life, so also does the Son give life to whomever he wishes. Nor does the Father judge anyone; he has committed the judgment of all to the Son, that all men may honor the Son just as they honor the Father. He who does not honor the Son does not honor the Father who sent him. Truly, truly, I tell you that he who hears my word and believes him that sent me has eternal life, and will never come into judgment, but has passed from death into life. Truly, truly, I tell you, the hour comes and now is when the dead will hear the voice of the Son of God, and they who hear will live. For as the Father has life in himself, he has also given the Son to have life in himself. He has given him authority to execute judgment because he is the Son of man. Stop marveling at this: the hour comes when all who are in the tombs will hear his voice and come forth—they who have practiced good to the resurrection of life, and they who have practiced evil to the resurrection of condemnation.

I can do nothing of myself. As I hear, I judge, and my judgment is righteous because I seek not my will but the will of him who sent me. If I testify of myself, my testimony is not true. But there is another who testifies of me, and I know that what he says of me is true. You sent to John. He testified to the truth. But I do not receive testimony from men; these things I say that you may be saved. He was a lamp that burns and shines, and you were willing to rejoice for an hour in his light. But I have a greater testimony than John's; the works which the Father gave me to accomplish, these works which I am doing, bear witness to me that the Father sent me. Besides this, the Father who sent me gives testimony about me. You have neither heard his voice at any time nor seen his form, and you do not have his word abiding in you, for you do not believe him whom he sent. You search the scriptures because you think to have eternal life through them, and these are testimonies about me. But you are not willing to come to me in order that you might have life. I do not receive glory from men, but I know that you do not have the love of God in you. I have come in the name of my Father, and you do not receive me; if another comes in his own name, you will receive him. How can you believe? You receive honor from one another and seek not the glory which is from the only God. Think not that I will accuse you to the Father. There is one who accuses you—Moses on whom you have set your hope. If you had believed Moses, you would have believed me, for he wrote about me. But if you will not believe his writings, how shall you believe my words?

Section 50. CONTROVERSY OVER PLUCKING GRAIN ON SABBATH

Mark 2:23-28.   Matthew 12:1-8.   Luke 6:1-5

One sabbath during that time, Jesus went through the grain fields. His disciples, becoming hungry, began to pull the heads of wheat along the way, rub them in their hands, and eat the wheat.

Some of the Pharisees saw it and began to say to him, Why do your disciples do what it is unlawful to do on the sabbath?

Jesus answered them, Have you never read what David did when he had need, when he and those with him became hungry? He entered the house of God when Abiathar was high priest and taking the loaves of shewbread, he ate and gave also to his companions, which it was not lawful for him or his companions to eat, but for the priests only? Or have you not read in the law that the priests profane the sabbath in the temple and are guiltless? I tell you that a greater thing than the temple is here. If you had known what it means: I will have mercy and not sacrifice; you would not have condemned the guiltless.

Then he continued, The sabbath came into being for the sake of man, and not man for the sabbath. Therefore the Son of man is lord also of the sabbath.

Section 51. THE HEALING OF A MAN WITH A WITHERED HAND

Mark 3:1-6.   Matthew 12:9-14.   Luke 6:6-11

He left them, and on another sabbath he entered their synagogue and began to teach. There was a man there whose right hand was withered. The scribes and Pharisees watched to see if he would heal him on the sabbath that they might find an accusation against him.

Knowing their thoughts, he said to the man with a withered hand, Rise up. Stand in the midst. He arose and stood up.

not a question

Then Jesus said to them, What man of you having one sheep, if he should fall into a ditch on the sabbath, would not lay hold of him and lift him up? How much more is a man worth than a sheep! Is it lawful to do good on the sabbath or to do evil, to save a life or to kill?

They kept still. Then he looked around on all of them with anger, being grieved at the hardness of their hearts, and said to the man, Stretch forth your hand.

He stretched it forth and it was restored whole to him as the other. But they were enraged and went out and took counsel with the Herodians against him, how they might destroy him.

CHAPTER VIII

CALL OF THE TWELVE AND THE SERMON
ON THE MOUNT

Section 52. The Spread of His Fame

Mark 3:7-12. Matthew 12:15-21

Jesus, when he knew this, retired with his disciples to the seashore where a vast multitude of people from Galilee, from Judea, from Jerusalem, from Idumea, from beyond the Jordan, and from the neighborhood of Tyre and Sidon followed him because they had heard what things he was doing. He told his disciples that a little boat should always stand by for him because of the crowd lest they should crush him, for he healed so many that all who had plagues kept crowding up to him that they might touch him. Also the unclean spirits, when they saw him, were falling down and crying out, You are the Son of God

But he admonished them repeatedly that they should not make him known.

This was so the word spoken through Isaiah the prophet might be fulfilled·

> Behold my servant whom I have chosen,
> My beloved in whom my soul is pleased;
> I will endue him with my Spirit,
> And he will proclaim judgment to the Gentiles.
>
> He will not strive nor cry aloud,
> Neither will anyone hear his voice in the streets;
> A bruised reed he will not break,
> Nor quench smoking flax,
> Until he sends forth judgment unto victory.
> In his name will the Gentiles rest their hope.

Section 53. Appointing the Twelve

Mark 3:13-19. Matthew 10:2-4. Luke 6:12-16

During these days, he went up into a mountain to pray and he spent the whole night in prayer to God. When day came, he called whom he wanted of his disciples and they came to him. He chose twelve and appointed them—them he also called apostles—that they should be with him and that he should send them forth to preach and to have authority to cast out demons.

The twelve whom he appointed were:

Simon to whom he gave the name of Peter;
Andrew his brother
James, the son of Zebedee and
John, his brother (to them he gave the name of
    Boanerges which means sons of thunder);

Philip;
Bartholomew;
Matthew, the tax-collector;
Thomas;
James, the son of Alphaeus;
Simon, the zealot;
Judas, the son of James who is also called Thaddaeus,[1] and
Judas Iscariot who became a traitor.

Section 54. The Sermon on the Mount

Matthew 5:1-8:1. Luke 6:17-49

A. The Setting

Matthew 5:1-2. Luke 6:17-20a

Then he went down with them and took his stand on a level place. There came to hear him and to be healed of their

---

1. A comparison of the list of apostles in the Synoptics shows that the same names are included in the same general order with the exception that Mark and Matthew have Thaddaeus, while Luke has Judas the son of James. It is to be supposed that this apostle had a double name (many did) and that while Luke gives one name, Mark and Matthew give the other.

diseases a great crowd of his disciples together with a great throng of people from all Judea and Jerusalem and the sea-coast of Tyre and Sidon. Those who were troubled with un-clean spirits were healed. And all the multitude sought to touch him, for power was coming out from him and he healed them all. When he saw the crowds, he went up into the mountain and when he himself had sat down his disciples came to him. Then he lifted up his eyes unto his disciples and opened his mouth and began to teach them.

ß. *The Beatitudes and Woes*

Matthew 5:3-12. Luke 6:20b-26

Blessed are they who feel their spiritual need, for theirs is the kingdom of heaven.

Blessed are they who are mourning now, for they will be comforted and will laugh.

Blessed are the meek, for they will inherit the earth.

Blessed are they who are hungering and thirsting for right-eousness, for they will be satisfied.

Blessed are the merciful, for they will have mercy shown to them.

Blessed are the pure in heart, for they will see God.

Blessed are the peacemakers, for they will be called the sons of God.

Blessed are they who have been persecuted on account of their uprightness, for theirs is the kingdom of heaven.

Blessed are you when men hate you and excommunicate you and revile you and spurn your name as evil and persecute you and speak all manner of evil against you falsely for the sake of the Son of man. Rejoice in that day, yes, leap for joy; for, lo, great is your reward in heaven; for their fathers did the same things to the prophets before you.

But woe to you who are rich! for you are receiving your comfort in full now.

Woe to you who are completely satisfied now! for you will hunger.

Woe to you who are laughing now! for you will mourn and weep.

Woe to you when all men speak well of you! for their fathers did the same to the false prophets.

C. Duties of Discipleship
Matthew 5:13-16

You are the salt of the earth; but if the salt should become tasteless, how can its saltiness be restored? It is good for nothing then but to be thrown out and walked on by men. You are the light of the world. A city sitting on a mountain cannot be hid. Neither do men light a lamp and put it under a measuring bucket, but upon a lampstand, and it gives light to all who are in the house. Let your light shine in like manner before men so that they may see your beautiful deeds and glorify your Father who is in heaven.

D. Christ's Ethical Standards
Matthew 5:17-20

Do not think that I came to destroy the law or the prophets. I came not to destroy but to complete. Truly, I tell you, until heaven and earth pass away, not one dash or comma will pass from the law until it all comes to pass. Whoever, therefore, breaks one of the least of these commandments and teaches men to do so will be called the least in the kingdom of heaven; but whoever practices and teaches them will be called great in the kingdom of heaven. For, I tell you, if your righteousness does not go far beyond that of the scribes and Pharisees, you will certainly not enter the kingdom of heaven.

E Jesus' Ethical Standards Illustrated

Matthew 5:21-48

You have heard that the ancients were told, You shall not murder, and, Whoever commits murder will be subject to judgment. But I tell you, everyone who continues to be angry with his brother will be subject to judgment. Yes, and whoever shall say to his brother, Raca, will be subject to the Sanhedrin; whoever shall say, You fool, will be subject to the hell of fire. If you, therefore, bring a gift to the altar and are reminded there that your brother has something against you, leave your gift before the altar. Go first and be reconciled to your brother; then come and offer your gift. Come to an agreement quickly with your opponent while you are still with him on the way to court lest he deliver you to the judge, and the judge to the attendant, and you be cast into prison. Surely, I tell you, you will not come out of there until you have paid the last penny.

You have heard that it was said, You shall not commit adultery. But I tell you that every one who looks at a woman with lust has already committed adultery with her in his heart. So if your right eye causes you to sin, pluck it out and throw it from you; for it is profitable for you that one of your members perish rather than have your whole body cast into hell. If your right hand causes you to sin, cut it off and throw it from you; it is profitable for you that one of your members perish rather than have your whole body cast into hell.

It has been said, Whoever divorces his wife, let him give her a certificate of divorce. But I tell you that every one who divorces his wife except for a matter of unchastity makes her an adulteress; and whoever marries her that is divorced commits adultery.

Again you have heard that it was said to the ancients, You shall not commit perjury, but shall perform your oaths to the Lord. But I tell you, Swear not at all: not by heaven, for it is the throne of God; nor by earth, for it is the footstool of his feet; nor by Jerusalem, for it is the city of the great king;

neither shall you swear by your head, for you cannot make one hair white or black.   But let your speech be a simple yes or no, for what is beyond these is of the evil one.

You have heard that it was said, An eye for an eye, and, A tooth for a tooth.   But I tell you, Resist not evil but turn your other cheek to him who slaps your right cheek.   Give your coat also to him who wishes to sue you and take away your shirt.   Go two miles with him who compels you to go one. Give to every one who asks of you.   Turn not away from him who wishes to borrow from you.   Ask not again from him who takes your things.

You have heard it said, Love your neighbor and hate your enemy.   But I tell you, Love your enemies; do good to them who hate you; bless them that curse you; pray for them who insult you.   Thus you will become the sons of your heavenly Father, the Most High.   For he causes his sun to shine upon the evil and the good; he sends the rain upon the righteous and the unrighteous.   If you love those who love you, what reward do you have?   Even tax-collectors and sinners love those who love them.   Or, if you greet only those who greet you, What are you doing more than others?   Even the Heathen do this, do they not?   Or, if you do good only to those who do good to you, what thanks have you?   Even sinners do the same thing. And, if you lend money to them from whom you expect to receive it, what thanks have you?   Even sinners lend to sinners that they may receive as much again in return.   Therefore, love your enemies; do good; and, lend, despairing of no man; and your reward will be great.   You will be perfect as your heavenly Father is perfect, for he is gracious to the unthankful and the evil.

F *Sincerity in Religious Acts*

Matthew 6:1-18

Be careful not to do your righteous acts before men to be seen of them. If you do, you will have no reward from your Father who is in heaven.

Therefore, whenever you make charitable gifts, do not sound a trumpet before you in the synagogues and streets as the hypocrites do that they may receive praise from men. Truly, I tell you, they have received their reward. But when you make charitable gifts, don't even let your left hand know what your right hand is doing that your charity may be in secret, and your Father who sees in secret will reward you.

Also, when you pray, do not be as the hypocrites are; for they love to pray while standing in the synagogues and on the street corners that they may attract the attention of men. Truly, I tell you, they have received their reward. But when you pray, go into your private room; shut the door; and pray to your Father which is in secret, and your Father who sees in secret will reward you.

While praying do not repeat empty words like the heathen do, for they think they will be heard because of much speaking. Do not be like them for your Father knows what you need before you ask. Pray, therefore, like this:

> Our Father who art in heaven,
> May thy name be revered,
> May thy kingdom come,
> May thy will be done,
> On earth as it is in heaven.
> Give us today our daily bread,
> And forgive us our debts,
> Even as we have forgiven our debtors.
> Do not let us be overcome by temptation,
> But deliver us from evil.[2]

2. Luke gives this model prayer under different circumstances (Luke 11:1–4). If we believe that it is given only once, Luke's position should be followed because: (1) Luke usually arranges the Q material in chronological order, while Matthew is not always careful to do so; (2) the setting in Luke is the more natural one for the giving of a model prayer; and, (3) its insertion here breaks into the logical arrangement of this paragraph on sincerity in religious activity. The same applies to the paragraph on worldly care and the one on asking and receiving (Matt. 6:19–34; 7:7–11) and the first two reasons are relevant. I have decided to leave Matthew's material in the body of the sermon because: (1) many scholars feel that we have in this material that which is repeated by Jesus under different circumstances, which is possible; and, (2) the sermon as recorded by Matthew has been regarded as a unit for so long that it should be broken up only on the basis of certain proof.

For if you forgive men their trespasses, your heavenly Father will forgive you; but if you refuse to forgive men, your Father will not forgive your trespasses.

Likewise, when you fast, do not be as the hypocrites—sad-faced; for they disfigure their faces so that they may appear to men to be fasting. I truly tell you, they have received their reward. But you, when you fast, anoint your head and wash your face that you may not appear as fasting to men but to your Father who is in secret; and your Father who sees in secret will reward you.

6   Worldly Ambition and Anxious Care
Matthew 6:19-34

Stop storing up for yourselves treasures upon the earth where moth and rust destroy and thieves break through and steal. Make a practice of storing up treasures for yourselves in heaven where neither moth nor rust destroys and where thieves do not break through nor steal. For where your treasure is, there will your heart be also.

The light of the body is the eye. If therefore your eye is sound, your whole body is full of light. But if your eye is bad, your whole body is full of darkness. Therefore, if the light which is in you is darkness, how great is that darkness! No one is able to be a slave to two masters; for he will hate one of them and love the other, or else he will be loyal to one of them and despise the other. You cannot be a slave to God and to mammon.

For this reason, I tell you, stop worrying about life; what you will eat, or drink; and about your body, what you will wear. Is not the life more than food and the body more than clothes? Consider the birds of heaven, they do not sow, neither reap, nor gather into granaries, and your heavenly Father feeds them. Do you not far surpass them? Which of you by worrying can add one hour to his days? And why do you worry about clothes? Consider the lilies of the field how they grow. They do not toil nor spin. But I tell you that even Solomon in all his splendor was not clothed like one of them. Since God clothes the grass of the field which today is and tomorrow is cast into the oven in this manner, shall he not much more clothe you, O you of little faith? Do not worry therefore saying, What shall we eat? or, what shall we drink? or, what shall we wear? For the heathen seek earnestly after all these things. Your heavenly Father knows that you have need of all these things. Continue to seek above all else the kingdom and his righteousness, and all these things will be added to you. Don't even worry about tomorrow, for tomorrow will have worries of its own. Sufficient unto the day is its own problems.

H Criticism Condemned
Matthew 7:1-6. Luke 6:37-42

Do not make a habit of judging lest you should be judged. For with the same judgment with which you judge, you will be judged; and with the same measure with which you measure, it will be measured unto you. Do not make a habit of condemning and you will not be condemned. Release and you will be released. Give and it will be given to you; good measure, pressed together, shaken down, and over-flowing will be given to your bosom.

Then he spoke a parable to them, Can a blind man be a guide to the blind? They will both fall into the pit, will they not? A disciple is not above his teacher, but each one will be as his teacher when he is fully trained.

Why do you stare at the splinter in your brother's eye and fail to perceive the board that is in your own eye? How can you say to your brother, Brother, let me pull the splinter out of your eye when you do not even see the board that is in your own eye? Hypocrite, first pull the board out of your own eye, and then you can see to pull the splinter out of your brother's eye.

Do not give what is holy to dogs nor cast your pearls before swine, lest they trample them under foot and having turned around rend you.

J   On Asking and Receiving
Matthew 7:7-11

Ask, and it will be given to you; seek, and you will find; knock, and it will be opened to you.   For everyone who asks receives; and he who seeks finds; and to him who knocks it will be opened.   What man of you will give his son a stone when he asks for bread?   or, when he asks for a fish will give him a serpent?   If you, therefore, who are evil know to give good gifts to your children, how much more will your Father in heaven give good things to those who ask him.

J   The Golden Rule
Matthew 7:12.   Luke 6:31

Therefore you ought to treat men just like you would want them to treat you for this sums up the Law and the Prophets.

K   The Sermon Concluded
Matthew 7:13 to 8:1.   Luke 6:43-49

Go in through the narrow gate, for wide is the gate and broad is the way which leads to destruction, and there are many who go in through it: for narrow is the gate and pressed-in the way which leads to life, and there are few who find it.

Beware of false prophets who come to you in sheep's clothing but are ravening wolves within.   From their fruits you will recognize them.   Men do not gather grapes from thornbushes, do they, nor figs from thistles?   Even so every good tree bears good fruit, and every decayed tree bears bad fruit.   A good tree does not and cannot bear bad fruit, nor a decayed tree good fruit. Every tree which does not bear good fruit is cut down and thrown into the fire. The good man out of the good treasure of his heart brings out the good, but the evil man out of the evil brings out evil; for out of the abundance of the heart the mouth speaks. So therefore, you will recognize them by their fruits.

Why do you call me, Lord, Lord, and do not the things which I say? Not every one who says to me, Lord, Lord, will enter into the kingdom of Heaven, but he who continues to do the will of my Father who is in heaven. Many will say to me in that day, Lord, Lord, have we not prophesied in thy name, and in thy name cast out devils, and in thy name performed many mighty things? Then will I confess to them, I never did know you; depart from me, you who are workers of iniquity.

Every one who comes to me, hears these words of mine, and practices them, I will show you what he is like. He is like the sensible man who in building his house, dug down, went deep, and placed the foundation on the rock. Then the rains fell, the winds blew, the flood came, and the rivers dashed against the house, but it did not fall, neither was it shaken, because it was built well and had been founded upon the rock.

But he who hears these words of mine and does not practice them will be compared to a foolish man who built his house upon the sand without a foundation, and the rains descended, the winds blew, and the rivers beat against that house and it fell right away and great was its ruin.

When Jesus had finished these words, the multitudes were astonished at his teaching, for he was teaching as one having authority and not as their scribes.

So when he came down from the mountain, great multitudes followed him.

CHAPTER IX

SPREAD OF INFLUENCE AND GROWTH OF HOSTILITY

Section 55. CENTURION'S SLAVE HEALED

Matthew 8:5-13.   Luke 7:1-10

Afterward he entered Capernaum. A Roman captain there had a slave who was dear to him and who was very ill, being at the point of death. When he heard about Jesus, he sent some Jewish elders to him to ask him to come and heal his slave. When they came to Jesus, they begged him earnestly, saying, He is worthy that you should do this favor for him; he loves our nation and has himself built the synagogue for us.

Jesus started with them.

When he was not far from the house, the captain sent some friends to him to say, Sir, do not trouble yourself, for I am not worthy that you should come under my roof; neither did I think myself worthy to come to you. But say the word, and my boy will be healed. I am a man put under authority, having soldiers under me also. I say to this one, Go, and he goes; and to another, Come and he comes; and to my slave, Do this, and he does it.

When he heard this, Jesus marveled at him; and turning to the crowd which followed him, he said, I tell you truly, I have not found so great faith, no, not in Israel. I tell you, many from the east and west will come and recline beside Abraham and Isaac and Jacob in the kingdom of Heaven, but the sons of the kingdom will be thrown out into the outer darkness where there will be weeping and gnashing of teeth.

When the messengers returned to the house, they found the slave well.[1]

---

1. Matthew and Luke give diverse accounts of this occurrence. Luke records the appeal as coming to Jesus through the Jewish elders and then through the friends of the captain who never personally appears. Matthew records it as coming directly from the captain himself. Of course, it may be said that what one does through another, he may truthfully be said to have done himself. This is the attitude adopted here though it does not solve the whole difficulty. However, the divergence is of small moment when compared to the central teaching of the incident, on which both writers are in full agreement.

Section 56. THE WIDOW'S SON RAISED

Luke 7:11-17

Soon afterward he went to a town called Nain, and his disciples, with a great multitude, were going along with him. Just as he approached the gate of the town, lo, a dead man was being carried out. He was the only son of his mother, and she a widow, and a considerable crowd was with her.

When he saw her, the Lord took pity on her and said, Stop weeping!

Then he came forward and touched the funeral couch, and the bearers stopped. He said, Young man, I say to you, Arise!

The dead man sat up and began to speak, and Jesus gave him to his mother. Then fear laid hold on them all, and they began to glorify God, saying, A great prophet has been raised in our midst, and, God has visited his people.

The report about him spread all over Judea and the surrounding country.

Section 57. JOHN IS PRAISED BY JESUS

Matthew 11:2-19.   Luke 7:18-35

John's disciples reported all these works of the Messiah to him while he was in prison. Calling two of his disciples, John sent them to the Lord saying, Are you the Coming One or are we to look for another?

When the men came to him, they said, John the Baptist sent us to you saying, Are you the Coming One or are we to look for another?

In that hour he healed many from diseases and plagues and evil spirits, and graciously gave sight to many blind men. Then he answered them, Go, report to John the things you have seen and heard: blind men are receiving their sight; the maimed are walking; the lepers are being cleansed; deaf men are hearing; dead men are being raised; the gospel is being preached to the poor; and, happy is the man who is not caused to sin by me.

When John's messengers had gone away, he began to speak to the crowds about John, What did you go out to the wilderness to see? a reed shaken by the wind? But what did you go out to see? a man clothed in soft garments? Lo, those who live in luxury and dress gorgeously are in royal palaces. But what did you go out to see? a prophet? Yes, I tell you, and far more than a prophet. This is he of whom it is written:

> Behold I send my messenger before your face,
> Who shall prepare your way before you.

I tell you truly, there is not one who is born of woman who is greater than John; nevertheless, he that is least in the kingdom of heaven is greater than he. But, from the days of John the Baptist until now, the kingdom of heaven is besieged, and violent men are grasping at it. For all the prophets as well as the law prophesied to John; and, if you will accept it, he is Elijah who was to come. Whoever has ears, let him hear. When the people and the tax-collectors heard him, they vindicated the righteousness of God, since they were baptized with the baptism of John. But the Pharisees and the lawyers frustrated God's purpose for them since they were not baptized by him. To what then shall I liken the men of this generation? What are they like? They are like children who sit in the market place and call to one another, saying:

> We piped to you, and you refused to dance;
> We lamented, and you refused to weep.

For John the Baptist came neither eating bread nor drinking wine, and you said, He has a demon. The Son of man has come both eating and drinking, and you say, Lo, a gluttonous man and wine drinker, a friend of tax-collectors and sinners. But wisdom is vindicated by all her children.

Section 58. The Anointing of Jesus

Luke 7:36-50

One of the Pharisees invited him to eat with him. He came into the house of the Pharisee and reclined at the table. Lo, a sinful woman of the city learning that he reclined in the house of the Pharisee came bearing an alabaster flask of perfume, took her stand behind him at his feet weeping, and began to wash his feet with her tears and dry them with the hair of her head, and she continued to kiss his feet and to anoint them with perfume.

When the Pharisee who had invited him saw this, he said to himself, If this man were really a prophet, he would have known who and what kind of woman this is who touches him—that she is a sinner.

Answering, Jesus said to him, Simon, I have something to say to you.

He said, Say on, Teacher.

A certain money-lender had two debtors. One owed him a hundred dollars and the other ten. Since neither had the money to pay, he graciously released them both. Which one of them will love him more?

Simon answered, I suppose the one to whom he forgave more.

He replied, You have judged correctly.

Then turning to the woman, he said to Simon, Do you see this woman? I came into your house; you gave me no water for my feet; she washed my feet with her tears and dried them with her hair. You gave me no kiss; she has not stopped kissing my feet since I came in. You did not anoint my head with oil; she anointed my feet with perfume. Therefore, I tell you, her many sins are forgiven because she loved much. But he to whom little is forgiven loves little.

He said to her, Your sins are forgiven.

Those who reclined with him began to say among themselves, Who is this who even forgives sins?

He said to the woman, Go in peace, your faith has saved you.

Section 59. ANOTHER TOUR OF GALILEE

Luke 8:1-3

Soon afterward he was traveling from city to city and from village to village preaching and proclaiming the good news of the kingdom of God. The twelve were with him as were also certain women who had been healed of evil spirits and diseases: Mary who is called Magdalene from whom seven demons had come out; Joanna the wife of Chuza, Herod's steward; Susanna; and, many other women—who were contributing to them out of their possessions.

Section 60. JESUS ACCUSED OF LEAGUE WITH BEELZEBUB

Mark 3:19-30

He went into a house and such a great crowd gathered together again that they could not even eat their meals. When his relatives heard it, they came to lay hold of him saying, He is out of his mind.

The scribes who had come down from Jerusalem kept saying, He has Beelzebub, and, By the prince of demons he is casting out demons.

Calling them to him, he began to speak to them in parables, How can Satan cast out Satan? If a kingdom is divided against itself, that kingdom cannot stand; and if a house is divided against itself, that house will not be able to stand. Likewise, if Satan rises up against himself and is divided, he cannot stand, but comes to an end.   No one is able to enter the house of a strong man and plunder his house unless he first bind the strong man.   Then he can really plunder his house.   Truly I tell you, All kinds of sin will be forgiven the sons of men, and their blasphemies which they blaspheme.   But whoever blasphemes the Holy Spirit has no forgiveness ever, but is guilty of eternal sin.

[He said this] because they kept saying, He has an unclean spirit.[2]

---

2. Luke also has an account of a like occurrence upon the entrance of Jesus into activities beyond Jordan.   Because of the differences of details and the usual chronological accuracy of both writers, these are treated as separate occurrences.   The question arises, however, as to which occasion Matthew records in chapter 12:22–37.   The language and details of Matthew's account is so like that of Luke that this writer has felt compelled to place it with Luke's account as coming from Q rather than Mark.

CHAPTER X

INTENSIFIED TEACHING BY JESUS AND THE TWELVE

Section 61. A Group of Parables Spoken by Seashore

Mark 4:1-34.   Matthew 13:1-35.   Luke 8:4-18

That same day, Jesus went out of the house and began to teach beside the sea.   Such a great multitude from every city resorted to him that he embarked in a boat and sat in it just off shore while the whole multitude stood on the beach up to the water's edge.   He began to teach them in many parables, saying to them as he taught:

Parable of the Soils

Mark 4:2-9.   Matthew 13:3-9.   Luke 8:5-8

Listen! a sower went out to sow his seed.   As he sowed, some seed fell by the wayside and were trodden under foot and the birds of heaven ate them.   Others fell upon the rocky ground where there was little depth of soil.   They sprang up at once because there was not much depth of soil, but when the sun began to shine, they were scorched because the soil was shallow and they had no moisture and were without root.   So they withered away.   Others fell in the midst of thorns.   The thorns grew up with them and choked them out so that they bore no fruit.   Others fell on good ground.   They grew and bore fruit, growing and increasing, some yielding a hundredfold, some sixty, and some thirty.

As he said these things, he cried out, He who has ears to hear, let him hear.

The Reason for the Parables

Mark 4:10-12.   Matthew 13:10-17.   Luke 8:9-10

When they were alone with him, the disciples and their companions asked him why he spoke to them in parables and what this parable meant.

He replied, To you it is given to know the mysteries of the kingdom of God. But it is not given to those others. Therefore, I speak to them in parables. For though they see, they will not see; and though they hear, they will not hear nor understand. In them is fulfilled the saying of the prophet Isaiah:

> You will hear with your ears,
> But you will not understand.
> You will see with your eyes,
> But you will not perceive.
> The heart of this people has become calloused;
> Their ears are dull of hearing;
> Their eyes also are closed;
> Lest they should ever perceive with their eyes,
> Hear with their ears,
> Understand with their hearts,
> And I turn back and heal them.

But your eyes are blessed, for they see; and your ears, for they hear. Truly, I tell you, many prophets and upright men have longed to see what you see and have not seen, and to hear what you hear and have not heard.

Explanation of the Parable of the Soils

Mark 4:13-20. Matthew 13:18-23. Luke 8:11-15

Do you not understand the parable of the sower? How then can you understand all the parables? The sower sows the seed which is the word of God. Those who hear the word and fail to understand it are the ones sown by the wayside. The devil comes at once and takes away the word sown among them for fear their heart will believe and they should be saved. Those that are sown on rocky ground are those who receive the word at once with joy as soon as they hear it. But they have no root in themselves and endure for only a little while. When tribulation comes, or persecution because of the word, they immediately are led to sin. Those which are sown among thorns are others who hear the word, but the anxieties of life, the deceitfulness of riches, the desire for the pleasures of life, and other things come in and choke out the word so that it bears no fruit. But those sown on good soil are those who hear the word with a good and sincere heart, understand it, and hold it fast. They will surely bear fruit in patience, some a hundred-fold, some sixty, and some thirty.

On the Use of Parables

Mark 4:21-25. Luke 8:16-18

He continued, No one lights a lamp and covers it with a bucket or puts it under a bed, does he? He sets it on a lamp-stand so that they who enter may see the light, does he not? There is nothing hidden except that it may be made manifest; neither is anything kept secret except that it may be revealed and come to light. If anyone has ears to hear, let him hear. Be careful how and what you hear. You will receive the same amount that you measure out and more too. For whoever has, it will be given to him and he will have an abundance. But whoever does not have, even what he has will be taken from him.

Parable of the Tares

Matthew 13:24-30

He set out another parable before them, saying, The king-dom of heaven is like a man who sowed good seed in his field. But while men slept, his enemy came and sowed wild wheat[1] in the midst of the wheat and went away. When the blades sprang up and bore fruit, the wild wheat also appeared. The slaves of the householder came and said to him, Sir, did you not sow good seed in your field? Where then does this wild wheat come from?

He said, An enemy has done this.

They said to him, Do you want us to go and gather them up?

---

1. A weed of Palestine which resembles wheat but is of no use.

He said, No, lest when you gather the wild wheat, you should also uproot the good wheat. Let them grow together until the harvest. Then I will tell the reapers, Gather first the wild wheat and tie it in bundles to be burned, but gather the good wheat into my granary.

The Seed Growing of Itself
Mark 4:26-29

Then he was saying, The kingdom of God is like this: suppose a man should cast seed upon the soil and then should sleep and rise night and day. The seed would sprout and grow up, but he knows not how. The soil automatically bears fruit; first the blade, then the ear, and then the full grain on the ear. When the grain is ripe, he immediately puts forth the sickle because the harvest has come.

The Mustard Seed
Mark 4:30-32.   Matthew 13:31-32

Again he said, How shall we compare the kingdom of God, or in what kind of parable shall we set it forth? It is like a grain of mustard seed which a man took and sowed in his field, which is the smallest of all the seeds of earth. But when it is sown, it springs up and grows greater than all the plants. It even becomes a tree and puts out great branches so that the birds of heaven can come and roost in its branches and under its shadow.

The Leaven
Matthew 13:33

He spoke another parable to them: the kingdom of heaven is like yeast which a woman took and worked into a bushel of flour until the whole was leavened.

Jesus' Custom of Speaking in Parables
Mark 4:33-34.   Matthew 13:34-35

So with many such parables Jesus kept speaking the word to the multitudes as they were able to hear it. He spoke nothing to them without a parable. This was so the word spoken through the prophet might be fulfilled, saying:

> I will open my mouth in parables;
> I will speak things which have been
>   hidden from the foundation of the world.

However, he explained all things to his disciples in private.

Section 62. His Mother and Brothers Seek Him

Mark 3:31-35.   Matthew 12:46-50.   Luke 8:19-21

While he was still speaking to the crowds, his mother and his brothers came up and since they could not get close to him because of the crowd, they stood outside and sent word that they wished to speak to him. The crowd was seated around him. Someone said, Lo, your mother and your brothers are outside wishing to see you.

He replied, Who is my mother?   and who are my brothers?

He looked around at those seated in a circle about him, stretched out his hand toward his disciples, and said, Look on my mother and my brothers. Whoever hears the word of God and does the will of my Father in heaven, the same is my brother and my sister and my mother.

Section 63. More Parables Spoken Privately
to the Disciples

Matthew 13:36-53

Explanation of the Parable of the Tares

Matthew 13:36-43

Then he left the multitudes and went into the house. His disciples came to him, saying. Explain to us the parable of the wild wheat in the field.

He replied, The one who sows the good seed is the Son of man. The field is the world. The good seed are the sons of the kingdom. The wild wheat are the sons of the Evil One. The enemy who sowed them is the Devil. The harvest is the consumation of the age. The reapers are the angels. Therefore, as the wild wheat is gathered up and burned with fire, so shall it be at the consumation of the age. The Son of man will send his angels to gather all causes of sin and those who practice wickedness out of his kingdom, and they will cast them into the furnace of fire where there will be the weeping and the gnashing of teeth. Then the upright will shine as the sun in the kingdom of their father. He who has ears to hear, let him hear.

Parable of the Hid Treasure

Matthew 13:44

The kingdom of heaven is like a treasure hidden in the field, which a man finding hid, and for joy went and sold all that he had and bought that field.

The Pearl of Great Price

Matthew 13:45-46

Again, the kingdom of heaven is like a trader seeking good pearls: when he finds one of great price, he goes and sells all that he has and buys it.

The Net

Matthew 13:47-50

Again, the kingdom of heaven is like a net which when it is cast into the sea gathers fish of every kind. When it is full, they draw it upon the beach, sit down, and gather the good into vessels; but the bad they cast out again. It will be like this at the consumation of the age. The angels will go forth and cut off the evil from the upright and cast them into the furnace of fire where there will be weeping and gnashing of teeth.

The Householder

Matthew 13:51-53

Have you understood all these things?

They answered, Yes.

He said to them, Therefore every scribe who has been made a disciple of the kingdom of heaven is like a man who is a householder. He brings forth out of his treasure things both new and old.

When Jesus had completed these parables he left that place.

Section 64. THE STILLING OF THE TEMPEST

Mark 4:35-41.   Matthew 8:18, 23-27.   Luke 8:22-25

On that same day when evening had come, he looked at the crowds around him and said to his disciples, Let us go to the other side.

His disciples followed him into a boat and they launched out along with other boats which accompanied him.   As they were sailing, he fell asleep.   Behold, a great wind storm arose on the sea so that the waves enveloped the boat; it was swamped, and they were in danger.   But he slept on in the stern of the boat on a cushion.

They woke him up and kept saying to him, Master, Master, do you not care that we perish?   Save us!

He replied, Why are you afraid?   Where is your faith?

Arising, he rebuked the winds and raging waters, and said to the sea, Peace, be still.

There was a great calm.

Then were they afraid with great fear and they marveled, saying to one another, What kind of man is this?   He even gives orders to the winds and the sea, and they obey him.

Section 65. The Healing of the Demoniacs

Mark 5:1-20.   Matthew 8:28-34.   Luke 8:26-39

They put in to the shore just across the sea from Galilee—at the country of the Gerasenes.   As soon as he left the boat and went ashore, two men with unclean spirits came out of the tombs to meet him.   For a long time they had worn no clothes nor lived in a house, but in the tombs.   No man could bind them anymore, no, not even with chains.   They had often been bound with chains and fetters, only to have the chains wrenched apart and the fetters broken in pieces by them.   No one was strong enough to tame them, For they were exceedingly fierce, so much so that no one dared to pass that way.   And throughout all the night and day they cried out and cut themselves with stones in the tombs and in the mountains.   When they saw Jesus from afar, they ran and worshipped him, crying out with a loud voice, What have we to do with you, Jesus, you Son of God the Most High?   Are you come to torment us before the time?   In God's name, we adjure you, do not torment us.

For he had commanded the unclean spirit to come out of the men, for it often seized them by force.

Jesus asked them, What is your name?

They replied, Legion: for we are many.   Then they began to beg him much that he would not command them to go into the abyss.   There was close by a herd of swine feeding in the mountain, and they begged him, If you cast us out, send us into the herd of swine.

He said to them, Go.

The demons entered into the swine, and lo, all the herd rushed down the precipice into the sea and were drowned. There were about two thousand.   The herdsmen fled into the city and the fields and told all the things which had happened to the men with unclean spirits.   And, lo, all the city came out to Jesus to see what had happened.   They found the men from whom the demons had departed sitting clothed and in their right mind at the feet of Jesus. So they were afraid. Then those who had seen it declared to them how it happened that these men were made well, and also about the swine.

Therefore all the people of the Gerasenes began to beg him to leave their land, for they were possessed with great fear. So he embarked in a boat.

One[2] of the men from whom the demons had gone out begged him that he might go with him.

But he sent him away, saying, Go home to your friends and tell them what things the Lord has done for you and how he had mercy on you.

He went away and began to publish in the city and in Decapolis the things Jesus had done for him, and all men marveled.

Section 66. A WOMAN HEALED AND A GIRL RAISED TO LIFE

Mark 5:21-43.   Matthew 9:18-26.   Luke 8:40-56

When Jesus had crossed over again in the boat to the other side, a great crowd welcomed him, for they were all waiting for him. While he was speaking to them by the sea, lo, one of the rulers of the synagogue named Jairus came and fell down at his feet and worshipped him, saying with much entreaty, My daughter is very ill and about to die. Will you not come to my house and lay your hands on her that she may be made whole and live?

She was his only daughter, being about twelve years old.

Jesus and his disciples went with him. As they went along, a great crowd followed and were pressing against him. A woman who had suffered for twelve years with a hemorrhage, had been subjected to much pain by many healers without being made better, but rather grew worse, and had spent all

---

2. Matthew records the healing of two demoniacs, while Mark and Luke only mention one. It is likely that the one mentioned by them became prominent and is therefore mentioned. The same thing is true of the healing of blind Bartimaeus.

that she had, having heard of Jesus, came up behind him in the crowd and touched the fringe of his garment. For she said to herself, If I can touch just his garment, I will be healed. At once the fountain of her blood was dried up and she knew in her body that she was healed of her plague.

Jesus knew instantly that power had gone out of him, and turning to the crowd, he said, Who touched my garment?

They all denied it. Peter and the disciples said to him, Master, you see the crowd pressing against you, and do you ask, Who touched me?

Jesus said, Someone touched me, for I felt power going out from me.

Then he looked around to see who had done this thing.

The woman, fearing and trembling, knowing what had happened to her, and seeing that she was not hidden, came and fell down before him and declared all the truth to him before all the people—why she had touched him and how she had been healed instantly.

He turned and said to her, Take courage, daughter, your faith has made you whole. Go in peace.

She was healed from that hour.

While he was still speaking, there came one from the house of the synagogue ruler, saying, Your daughter has died. Why do you continue to trouble the teacher?

Jesus overheard the words and said to the ruler, Be not afraid. Only believe, and she will recover.

When he came to the house, he would permit no one to go in with him except Peter, James, John the brother of James, and the father and mother of the girl. When Jesus entered the house of the ruler, he saw flute players and the crowd making a tumult, for they were all weeping and wailing over her. He said to them, Why do you make a tumult and weep? Give way! The girl has not died but is sleeping.

They ridiculed him, knowing that she had died.

When the crowd had gone out, he took the father and the mother of the child and those who were with him and came in where the child was. He took her hands and said, Talitha Cuma (which interpreted is, Little girl, I say to you, Rise up).

Her spirit returned instantly and she got up and walked about. He commanded them to give her something to eat.

Her parents were greatly amazed, and though he charged them much to tell this to no man, the report of it went out into all the land.

Section 67. Two Blind Men Healed and a Demon Cast Out

Matthew 9:27-34

As Jesus passed from thence, two blind men began to follow along and cry out, Son of David, have mercy on us.

When he came into the house, the blind men came to him; Jesus said to them, Do you believe that I can do this?

They said, Yes, Lord.

He touched their eyes and said, Let it be to you according to your faith.

Their eyes were opened.

Then Jesus charged them, saying, See that you let no man know about it.

But they went out and spread his fame throughout all that country.

As they were going out, a dumb man, possessed by a demon, was brought to him. When the demon was cast out, the dumb man began to speak. The multitude marveled, saying, the like of this has never been seen in Israel.

But the Pharisees continued to say, He is casting out demons by the prince of demons.

Section 68. JESUS AGAIN VISITS NAZARETH

Mark 6:1-6a.   Matthew 13:54-58.   John 4:44

He left that place and came into his native country;[3] his disciples followed him.   When the sabbath came, he began to teach them in the synagogue.   The many who heard him were amazed, saying, Where did this one get all these things? and, what is the wisdom that is given to him, that such powers are wrought by his hands?   Is not this the carpenter, the son of a carpenter?   Is not his mother named Mary and his brothers James and Joseph and Simon and Jude?   Are not his sisters all here with us?

So they were caused to stumble at him.

Jesus said to them, A prophet is not without honor except in his own neighborhood, among his own kindred, and in his own house.

Therefore he could not do many mighty works there, nothing except laying his hands on a few sick people and healing them. And he was wondering at their unbelief.

Section 69. THE TWELVE SENT OUT: A TOUR OF GALILEE

Mark 6:6-13. Matthew 9:35 to 10:1; 10:5-15; 10:40 to 11:1
Luke 9:1-6

Jesus made a tour of all the cities and villages, teaching in their synagogues, proclaiming the gospel of the kingdom, and healing all kinds of disease and infirmity.   When he saw the multitudes, he was moved with pity for them because they were distressed and wandering as sheep having no shepherd.

---

3. Luke also has an account of a visit to Nazareth which takes place at the very beginning of the Galilean campaign.   Besides the possibility that Jesus would make more than one effort to win the allegiance of his own townspeople, the internal evidence points strongly to two different visits rather than one.   In Luke, the address of Jesus so angers the people that they seek to kill him, while there seems no place for this in Matthew and Mark.   In Luke, he is expected to work miracles, while in this account he can work only a few because of their unbelief.

Then he said to his disciples, The harvest is truly abundant, but the laborers are few. Pray the lord of the harvest therefore to send out laborors into his harvest.

Then he called his twelve disciples together[4] and gave them power and authority over unclean spirits so they could cast them out and heal all kinds of disease and sickness. After which he began to send them out two by two to proclaim the kingdom of God and to heal. Jesus charged them, saying, Go not into the way of the Gentiles nor enter into any city of the Samaritans. Go rather to the lost sheep of the house of Israel. As you go, preach, saying, The kingdom of heaven has come near. Heal those who are sick. Raise those who are dead. Cleanse the lepers. Cast out the demons. You have received without pay. Give without pay.

He commanded them, Take nothing for the journey except a staff only: no bread, no wallet, no gold, no silver. Neither shall you take two shoes nor two coats, but go shod in sandals, for the worker deserves his food. When you enter a city or a village, search out one in it who is deserving and stay in his house until you leave. As you enter the house, greet him; and if the house is deserving, let your peace come upon it. But if it is not worthy, let your peace come back to you. When a place will not receive you nor listen to your words, shake off the dust that is under your feet as a testimony against them as you leave that place. I tell you truly, it will be more endurable for the land of Sodom and Gomorrah in the day of judgment than for that city. He who receives you, receives me; and he who receives me, receives him that sent me. He that receives a prophet in the name of a prophet will receive a prophet's reward. He who receives an upright man in the name of an upright man will receive the reward of an upright man. But he who gives

4. In this charge, Matthew gives a far more extended statement than does either Luke or Mark. It seems that he gathered into one discourse all the material which Jesus set forth as involving the duty of Christian preachers. He does not record the subsequent sending of the seventy. We have decided, therefore, that most of Matthew 10 is to be placed in its order as given by Luke. This does not, of course, change our evaluation of the authenticity of this material. Matthew wanted to make this chapter a full report of all that Jesus said to the apostles about their work and gathered his material from all sections of the ministry of Jesus.

one of these little ones only a cup of water in the name of a disciple, I tell you truly, he will not lose his reward.

Then they departed and went through the villages, preaching the gospel and saying that men should repent. They also cast out many demons and anointed with oil many that were sick and healed them on every hand.

When Jesus had finished instructing his twelve disciples, he went away to teach and preach in their cities.

Section 70. HEROD THINKS THAT JESUS IS JOHN THE BAPTIST

Mark 6:14-29.   Matthew 14:1-12.   Luke 9:7-9

It was at that time that Herod the Tetrarch heard the report concerning Jesus and all the things which had happened, for his name had become well known.   He was troubled, for some said that John the Baptist had risen from the dead, and some that Elijah had appeared, but others that he was a prophet like one of the ancient prophets.

Herod said, I beheaded John.   Who then is this one about whom I hear such things?   Surely John the Baptist has risen from the dead and thus these powers work through him.   So he was seeking to see him.

Now Herod himself had sent and seized John and bound him in prison for the sake of Herodias, his brother Philip's wife, because he had married her.   For John had repeatedly said to Herod, It is not lawful for you to have the wife of your brother.   This had caused Herodias to have a grudge against him so that she wanted to kill him, but she could not.   Herod feared John, knowing that he was an upright and holy man, and that the multitudes counted him as a prophet.   Therefore he kept him safe and hearing him was much perplexed, but he heard him gladly.

But an opportunity came.   When Herod made a supper on his birthday for his nobles and captains and the chief men of

Galilee, the daughter of Herodias came and danced in their midst.   Herod was pleased as were those who reclined with him. So the king said to the girl, Ask of me anything that you desire, and I will give it to you.   He even said on oath, Ask me anything that you desire and I will give it to you even to half of my kingdom.

Going out, she said to her mother, What shall I ask?

She said, The head of John the Baptist.

She then made haste to come in to the king and made her request, saying, I want you to give me the head of John the Baptist on a platter at once.

At this the king became very sad; but for the sake of his oath and those who reclined with him, he would not refuse her Therefore, the king sent out an attendant with orders to bring in his head.   He went and beheaded him in prison, brought his head on a platter, and gave it to the girl; and the girl gave it to her mother.

When his disciples heard it, they came and took up his corpse and put it in a tomb.   Then they came and told Jesus.

CHAPTER XI

SPECIAL TRAINING OF THE TWELVE

Section 71. FEEDING THE FIVE THOUSAND

Mark 6:30-44. Matthew 14:13-21. Luke 9:10-17. John 6:1-13

The apostles came back and told Jesus all that they had done and taught. He said to them, Come away into a solitary place and rest a while.

For many were coming and going, and they could not even find time to eat. Therefore they departed in a boat to the other side of the Sea of Galilee, which is Tiberias, to a desert place near Bethsaida. But many saw them going and knew them, so a great crowd from all the neighboring cities followed him because they had seen the signs which he performed on the sick. They ran together on foot and arrived before them.

Jesus and his disciples went up on a hill. (It was near the Passover, the feast of the Jews). When therefore he lifted up his eyes, he saw the great crowd, and his heart was moved with pity for them because they were like sheep without a shepherd. So he began to teach them many things about the kingdom of God and to heal their sick.

When it became late in the evening, his disciples came and said to him, This is a desert place and the hour is late. Send the crowd away so they can disperse and go to the farms and villages near by and buy something to eat.

He said, They have no need to go away. You give them something to eat. To Philip he said, Where can we buy bread for these to eat? (This he did to test him, for he himself already knew what he was going to do).

Philip answered him, Forty dollars' worth would not be enough for each one to have a little bit of bread.

They said, Shall we go and buy forty dollars' worth of bread that we may give them food?

He said, How much bread do you have? Go and see.

One of the disciples—Andrew, the brother of Simon Peter—said to him, There is a lad here who has five barley loaves and two little fish. But what are they among so many?

Jesus said to the disciples, Have them recline in groups of fifty or a hundred.

There was much grass there, so they all reclined on the green grass in groups. He, taking the five loaves and two fish, lifted his eyes to heaven and gave thanks. Then, having broken the loaves, he gave them to the disciples to distribute to the crowd. Likewise the fish.

They did all eat and were satisfied. The number which ate was about five thousand men besides the women and children.

He said to the disciples, Gather up the left over pieces that nothing go to waste.

They took up twelve baskets full of pieces and of the fish.

Section 72. THE PEOPLE PREVENTED FROM TRYING TO MAKE JESUS A KING

Mark 6:45-46. Matthew 14:22-23. John 6:14-15

When the people, therefore, saw the sign which he did, they began to say, Surely this is the Prophet who is coming into the world.

He made the disciples embark at once in the boat and go on before him to the other side, to Bethsaida, while he dismissed the crowd.

Because Jesus knew that they were about to come and make him a king by force, he dismissed the crowd and went away alone to a hill to pray.

Section 73. JESUS WALKS ON THE SEA BY NIGHT

Mark 6:47-52. Matthew 14:24-33. John 6:16-21

When evening came, he was there alone, but the disciples were already in the middle of the sea on their way to Capernaum. Even when it became dark, Jesus had not come to them. The sea became very rough because of a great wind which blew. He saw that they were distressed in rowing, so when they had rowed about three or four miles, it being the fourth watch of the night, Jesus came to them, walking on the waters.

When the disciples saw him walking on the sea, they were terror-stricken and cried out from fear, It is a ghost.

He immediately spoke to them, saying, Take courage. Stop being afraid. It is I.

Peter said, Lord, since it is you, tell me to come to you on the water.

He replied, Come on.

Peter descended from the boat and walked on the water toward Jesus. But when he looked at the wind, he became afraid and began to sink. He cried out, Lord, save me!

Immediately, Jesus put out his hands and took hold of him, saying, O you of little faith, why did you doubt?

Then they received him into the boat; and when they had gone up into the boat, the wind stopped. Those in the boat began to worship him, saying, You are surely the Son of God.

However, they were greatly amazed, for they did not understand the lesson of the loaves, their hearts being dull.

The boat come to the land where they were going.

Section 74. THE RECEPTION AT GENNESARET

Mark 6:53-56.   Matthew 14:34-36

When they had moored to land, they came to Gennesaret.[1] The men of that place knew him when he came out of the boat. So they began to send to the whole surrounding country, and the people began to bring all who were sick to the place where he was on their pallets.   Wherever he entered into the villages, cities, or the country side, they laid the sick in the market places and begged him just to let them touch the hem of his garments.   Whoever touched him was healed.

Section 75. DISCOURSE ON THE BREAD OF LIFE

John 6:22-71

The people who had remained on the other side of the sea had seen that there was only one boat there, and that Jesus had not entered it with his disciples, but had sent them away by themselves in the boat.   However, the next day when other boats came from Tiberias and put in near the place where they had eaten bread after the Lord had given thanks and the multitude saw that neither Jesus nor his disciples were there, they themselves entered into the boats and came to Capernaum seeking Jesus.   When they found him on the other side of the sea, they said to him, Rabbi, when did you get here?

Jesus answered them, I tell you truly, you are not seeking me because you saw signs, but because you ate the loaves and were filled.   Stop laboring for perishing food but for the food which endures unto eternal life, which the Son of man will give you; for God the Father has certified him.

They said therefore to him, What are we to do that we may keep working the works of God?

---

1. Since Mark and Matthew do not give an account of the discourse at Capernaum on this day, this paragraph is to be taken as a summary account of the ministry of Jesus for the next several weeks.

Jesus answered them, This is the work of God: to believe in him whom he sent.

Then they said to him, What sign are you going to do so that we may see it and believe you? What do you work? Our forefathers ate the manna in the desert, as it is written:

He gave them bread from heaven to eat.

Jesus answered them, Truly, truly, I say to you, Moses did not give you the real bread from heaven, but my Father gives you the true bread from heaven. The bread of God is that which comes down out of heaven and gives life to the world.

They said to him, Lord, always give us this bread.

Jesus answered them, I am the bread of life. He that comes to me will never hunger, and he that believes in me will never thirst. But, as I told you, you have seen me, yet you do not believe. Everyone whom the Father gives me comes to me, and he who comes to me I will never cast out, for I have come down out of heaven, not to do my will but the will of him who sent me. This is the will of him who sent me, that I should lose none of what he has given me, but raise it up on the last day. This is the will of my Father, that everyone who sees the Son and believes in him shall have eternal life, and I will raise him on the last day.

Then the Jews began to grumble at him because he said, I am the bread which came out of heaven; and they were saying, Is not this Jesus the son of Joseph? Do we not know his father and mother? How now does he say, I have come down from heaven?

Jesus answered them, Stop grumbling among yourselves. No one is able to come to me except the Father who sent me draw him, and I will raise him on the last day. It is written in the prophets:

They shall all be taught by God. Everyone who has listened to the Father so as to learn will come to me. Not that anyone has seen the Father, except him who is from God; he has seen the Father. I tell you truly, he who believes has eternal life. I am the bread of life. Your forefathers ate the manna in the wilderness, but they died. This is the bread which came down out of heaven that anyone who eats it should never die. I am the living bread which came down from heaven. If anyone shall eat of this bread, he will live forever. The bread which I give is my flesh, given for the life of the world.

The Jews kept disputing with one another, saying, How can this man give us his flesh to eat?

Jesus said to them, I tell you truly, Except you eat the flesh of the Son of man and drink his blood, you have no life within you. He who continues to eat my flesh and drink my blood has eternal life, and I will raise him up on the last day. My flesh is real food, and my blood is real drink. He who continues to eat my flesh and drink my blood continues to live in me and I in him. Just as the living Father sent me and I live because of the Father, so also he who continues to eat me will live because of me. This is the bread which came down from heaven; your forefathers ate and died; he who continues to eat this bread will live forever.

He said these things while he was teaching in the synagogue at Capernaum.

On hearing them, many of his disciples said, This is a hard saying. Who is able to hear it?

Jesus, knowing within himself that his disciples were grumbling because of this, said to them, Does this scandalize you? What if you should see the Son of man ascending to where he was before? The Spirit gives life; the flesh does not help at all. The words which I have spoken to you are spirit and life. But there are some of you who do not believe. (For Jesus knew from the beginning who they were who did not believe and who it was that would betray him.) So he said, Because of this I said to you, No one can come to me except him to whom it is given by the Father.

Upon this, many of his disciples turned back and walked with him no more.

Jesus therefore said to the twelve, You do not wish to go away too, do you?

Simon Peter answered him, Lord, to whom would we go? You have the words of eternal life. We have come to believe and to be certain that you are the Holy One of God.

Jesus answered them, Have I not chosen Twelve? Yet, one of you is a devil.

He was referring to Judas, the son of Simon Iscariot, one of the twelve, for he was going to betray him.

Section 76. A QUESTION ABOUT CEREMONIAL DEFILEMENT

Mark 7:1-23.   Matthew 15:1-20.   John 7:1

After this, Jesus walked in Galilee; he did not wish to walk in Judea, because the Jews were seeking to kill him.

Then some Pharisees and scribes from Jerusalem came to Jesus. They noticed that some of his disciples were eating with defiled (that is, unwashed) hands. (For the Pharisees and all the Jews will not eat until they wash their hands up to the elbow in obedience to the tradition of the elders; and when they come from the market place, they do not eat until they have bathed[2]; and they have to keep a number of other traditions about washing cups and pots and basins.) So the Pharisees and scribes asked him, Why do your disciples disobey the tradition of the elders? They eat bread with defiled hands and do not wash them.

He answered them, You hypocrites, well did Isaiah prophesy, saying, as it is written:

---

2. Because the textual evidence is about evenly balanced, and because "bathed" seems more in harmony with the practice of the Jews, this reading is adopted instead of "sprinkled."

> This people honors me with their lips,
> But their heart is far from me.
> In vain do they worship me,
> For they teach the precepts of men as doctrine.

You leave the commandments of God to hold on to the traditions of men.

He continued, Thus you ignore God's commandments that you may keep your own traditions. God said, Honor your father and your mother, and, He who speaks evil of father or mother, let him die the death. But you say, Whoever says to his father or mother, Corban (It is a gift); everything I have by which you might have been helped is Corban, you no longer let him do anything to honor his father and mother. Thus you nullify the law of God by your traditions which you deliver. You do many such things.

Then he called the crowd to him again and said to them, All of you listen to me and understand. There is nothing outside a man which by entering into his mouth can defile him. The thing that defiles a man is what comes out of his mouth.

When he had come into the house with his disciples apart from the crowd, they said to him, Do you know that the Pharisees were scandalized when they heard your word?

He answered, Every plant which my heavenly Father does not plant will be rooted up. Let them alone. They are blind guides. If a blind man guides a blind man, they will both fall into the pit.

Peter said to him, Explain the parable to us.

He said, Are you also still without perception. Do you not see that nothing which enters the mouth from the outside can defile a man because it does not enter his heart but his stomach, and then goes out into the waste? (So he made all foods clean.) The things which defile a man are those things that come out of his mouth, for they come from the heart. Out of the heart come evil thoughts, murders, adultery, immorality, stealing, false witnessing, blasphemy, covetings, slander, deceit, sensuality, malice, arrogance, and foolishness. All these evil things come out of a man, and they defile him. But eating with unwashed hands does not defile anyone.

Section 77. JESUS HEALS THE DAUGHTER OF A GREEK WOMAN

Mark 7:24-30.   Matthew 15:21-28

Jesus left there and withdrew into the territory of Tyre and Sidon. He entered a house and wanted no one to know it, but he could not keep it secret. Lo, a Canaanite woman of that district hearing of him, coming out, fell down at his feet, pleading with him, Lord, Son of David, have mercy on me. My daughter is suffering horribly with a demon.

He did not even answer her, for she was a Greek, a Syro-Phoenician by birth.

His disciples came and kept saying, Send her away for she cries out after us.

He replied, I am not sent except to the lost sheep of the house of Israel.

But she came and worshipped him, saying, Lord, help me.

He said to her, Let the children be first satisfied. It is not right to take the children's bread and throw it to the dogs.

She said, True, Lord, but even the dogs eat the crumbs that fall from the master's table.

Then Jesus answered her, Woman, you have a great faith. Let your wish be granted. Go. The demon has gone out of your daughter.

She then departed to her own house. There, she found the little girl lying on the bed, the demon having gone out.

Section 78. JESUS HEALS MANY AND FEEDS FOUR THOUSAND

Mark 7:31 to 8:9.   Matthew 15:29-38

Then Jesus, leaving the neighborhood of Tyre, came by the way of Sidon to the Sea of Galilee, passing through the district of Decapolis.   Here, they brought a deaf and dumb man to him and were begging him to lay his hands on him.   He took him aside from the crowd and put his fingers into his ears. Having spat, he touched his tongue.   Then looking up to heaven, he sighed, and said to him, Ephphatha (that is, Be opened).

The man's ears were opened and his tongue loosed, and he began to speak clearly.   Then he forbade them to tell anyone about it; but the more he forbade them, the more eagerly they made it public.

Then he went up into a mountain and was sitting there. But a great multitude came, having with them the lame, the blind, the dumb, the maimed, and many others.   These they put at his feet and he made them well.   When the crowd saw the dumb speak, the deaf made to hear, the maimed whole, the lame walking, and the blind seeing they were greatly amazed and glorified the God of Israel, saying, He has done all things well.

Since the multitude had nothing to eat, he called his disciples to him and said, My heart is moved with pity for the multitude, for they have already stayed three days with me with nothing to eat.   If I send them away to their homes fasting, they may faint in the way, and some of them are from afar.

The disciples replied, Where can we get enough bread to fill such a crowd here in the desert?

Jesus said to them, How much bread do you have?

They said, Seven loaves and a few small fish.

He commanded the crowd to recline on the ground.   He took the seven loaves, gave thanks, broke them, and gave to the

disciples to distribute. They gave them to the multitude.
Then he took the small fish and blessed them. These he also
told them to distribute.

All of them—about four thousand men besides women and
children—ate and were satisfied. They also took up seven
baskets full of pieces which were left over.

Section 79. JESUS REFUSES A SIGN

Mark 8:10-12.   Matthew 15:39 to 16:4

When he had dismissed the multitude, he embarked in a
boat with his disciples and came into the district of Dalmanutha.
The Pharisees and Sadducees came up and began to argue with
him.   To test him, they requested that he should show them a
sign from heaven.

He gave a deep and troubled sigh and said, When it is
evening, you say, Fair weather, for the sky is red.   In the morning, Stormy weather today, for the sky is red and overcast.
You know how to read the face of the sky, but you cannot read
the signs of the times.[3]   An evil and adulterous generation
seeks a sign, but no sign will be granted it except the sign of
Jonah.

Then he left them and went away.

Section 80. WARNINGS AGAINST TEACHINGS OF
PHARISEES AND SADDUCEES

Mark 8:13-26.   Matthew 16:5-12

He entered a boat and went again to the other side.   But
they forgot to take bread and had only one loaf with them in
the boat.

---

3. A. B. Bruce, "The Synoptic Gospels," *Expositor's Greek Testament*, ed. W. R. Nico
(Grand Rapids, Michigan: Wm. B. Eerdmans Publishing Company, n.d.), p. 219, says, "Vv.
1 and 3, though not in B and bracketed by W.H., may be regarded as part of the text."

He began to warn them, saying, Take heed; beware of the leaven of the Pharisees and Sadducees and the leaven of Herod.

They began to discuss it with one another and said, It is because we have taken no bread.

Jesus, knowing, said, Why do you reason among yourselves that it is because you have taken no bread, Oh you of little faith. Do you not know nor understand? Have your hearts been dulled? You have eyes, can you not see? You have ears, can you not hear? Do you remember how many pieces you took up when I broke five loaves among the five thousand?

They said to him, Twelve baskets full.

How many baskets of pieces did you take up when I broke seven loaves among the four thousand?

They said, Seven.

He said to them, How is it then that you do not know that it is not concerning bread that I speak to you? But beware of the leaven of the Pharisees and Sadducees.

Then they understood that he did not tell them to beware of the leaven of bread, but of the teachings of the Pharisees and Sadducees.

They came to Bethsaida. There, they brought a blind man to him and begged him to touch him. But he took hold of the blind man's hands, led him outside the city, spat upon his eyes, laid his hands on him, and asked, Can you see?

He looked up and said, I see men walking, but they look like trees.

Once again he put his hands on his eyes. Then he looked steadily and was restored, and he saw everything clearly. Jesus sent him home, saying, Do not even go into the village.

Section 81. THE GREAT CONFESSION AT CAESAREA PHILIPPI

Mark 8:27-30.   Matthew 16:13-20.   Luke 9:18-21

Jesus and his disciples came into the district of Caesarea Philippi.   On the way, while he was praying alone, they came to him.   He asked them, Who do men say that I, the Son of man, am?

They answered, Some say, John the Baptist; others, Elijah; but others, Jeremiah or one of the ancient prophets come to life

He asked them, But you, who do you say I am?

Simon Peter answered, You are the Messiah, the Son of the living God.

Jesus answered him, Blessed are you, Simon, son of John, for flesh and blood did not make you know this, but my Father who is in heaven.   I tell you that you are a stone (i.e., Peter) and upon this rock I will build my church.   The gates of Hades will never prevail against it.   I give you the keys of the kingdom of heaven.   Whatever you bind on earth will have been bound in heaven, and whatever you loose on earth will have been loosed in heaven.

Then he warned the disciples and told them not to tell that he was the Messiah.

Section 82. JESUS PROPHESIES HIS DEATH

Mark 8:31 to 9:1.   Matthew 16:21-28.   Luke 9:22-27

From that time on, Jesus began to teach his disciples and show them that it was necessary for the Son of man to go up to Jerusalem, to suffer many things, to be rejected by the elders and chief priests and the scribes, to be put to death, and to rise again after three days.   He continued speaking this word plainly.

But Peter took him aside and began to rebuke him, saying, May God forbid you, Lord; this shall never be your lot.

He turned and said to Peter, Get behind me, Satan. You are a hindrance to me, for your conception of things is not God's but man's.

Then Jesus called the crowd and his disciples and said, If any man desires to come after me, he must deny himself, take up his cross daily, and keep following me. Whoever desires to save his life will lose it, but whoever loses his life for my sake and the gospel's will find it. What does a man gain if he obtains the whole world and loses his own life? What would a man give in exchange for his life?

The Son of man is coming in the glory of his Father and with his holy angels. Then he will give to every one according to his deeds. Whoever shall be ashamed of me and my words in this adulterous and sinful generation, the Son of man will be ashamed of him when he comes.

I tell you of a truth, there are some who stand here who will not taste death till they see the Son of man coming in the kingdom of God with power.

Section 83. The Transfiguration of Jesus

Mark 9:2-13. Matthew 17:1-13. Luke 9:28-36

A week after these words,[4] Jesus took Peter, James, and John his brother apart, and went up into a high mountain to pray. While he was praying, he was transfigured before them. His face was changed and shone like the sun. His garments became brilliantly white like no fuller on earth can whiten. And, lo, two men appeared and were speaking to him—Moses and Elijah. Who, when they appeared in glorious fashion, began to speak to him of his exodus which he was going to accomplish in Jeru-

---

4. Mark says six days; Luke, eight. A week would allow for six intervening days, and if the two terminal days were counted, would make eight days. Therefore, there is no serious discrepancy between the two accounts.

salem. Peter and his companions were heavy-eyed with sleep. But they awoke and saw his glory and the two men who were standing with him.

When they went away, Peter said to Jesus, Master, it is good for us to be here. Let us build three booths: one for you, one for Moses, and one for Elijah.

For he did not know what he was saying, because they were greatly afraid.

Even while he spoke, a cloud came and enveloped them, and they were terrified when the cloud came. A voice came out of the cloud, saying, This is my beloved Son in whom I am well pleased. Listen to him!

When the disciples heard it, they fell upon their faces stricken with terror. But Jesus came and touched them and said, Arise. Stop being afraid.

Then they lifted up their eyes and looked around, but they no longer saw anyone except Jesus.

On the way down the mountain, Jesus commanded them, Do not tell the things that you have seen until the Son of man shall have risen from the dead.

So they kept silence and told no one in those days what they had seen. But they questioned one another about what the resurrection from the dead might be.

They asked him, Why then do the scribes say that Elijah must come first?

He said to them, Elijah does come first to restore all things. I tell you that Elijah has already come, but they did not recognize him, and did everything they wished to him just as it is written of him. Likewise it is written of the Son of man that he must suffer many things and be despised by them.

Then the disciples understood that he referred to John the Baptist.

Section 84. JESUS HEALS AN EPILEPTIC BOY
Mark 9:14-29.   Matthew 17:14-21.   Luke 9:37-42

Next day, they came down from the mountain and found a great crowd gathered around the disciples, and the scribes arguing with them. When the crowd saw him, they marveled and ran to greet him.

He asked them, Why do you argue with them?

Lo, a man from the crowd fell down before him and cried out, Teacher, I beg you to look at my son and have mercy on him, for he is my only child. He is an epileptic, and a dumb spirit seizes him. Wherever it takes him, he cries out, and it convulses him. Then he foams and grinds his teeth, and he is fading away. It hardly ever leaves him, and sometimes he falls into the fire, and sometimes in the water. He suffers continually. I brought him to your disciples and begged them to cast it out, but they could not heal him.

Jesus answered, Oh unbelieving and perverse generation, how long shall I be with you? How long must I endure you? Bring your son to me.

While he was coming, the spirit caught sight of Jesus and immediately tore him and put him in convulsions. The boy fell down and rolled on the earth, foaming at the mouth. He asked his father, How long has he been like this?

He said, From childhood. But if you are able, have pity on us and help us.

Jesus said, If you are able? All things are possible to him who believes.

The father of the boy cried out immediately, I believe. Help my unbelief.

Jesus saw that the crowd was running together, so he rebuked the unclean spirit and commanded him, You deaf and dumb spirit, I command you, come out of him and enter in him no more.

He cried out, convulsed him much, and then came out.

He became as dead, so that many said, He is dead.

But Jesus took him by the hand and raised him up, and he stood. Thus he healed him in that hour and restored him to his father. They were all amazed at the majesty of God.

When he had entered a house, his disciples asked him privately, Why could we not cast it out?

He said to them, Because of the smallness of your faith, for this kind cannot come out except by prayer. I tell you of a truth, if you have faith as great as a grain of mustard, you can say to this mountain, Be removed from here to there, and it will be removed, and nothing will be impossible to you.

Section 85. JESUS AGAIN FORETELLS HIS DEATH

Mark 9:30-32.   Matthew 17:22-23.   Luke 9:43-45

While they all marveled at the things which he did, they returned from that place and began to travel through Galilee, but he did not want anyone to know it. While they were going about Galilee, Jesus kept repeating these words to them: Store up these words in your ears. The Son of man is going to be delivered up into the hands of men, and they will put him to death, but he will rise again after being dead three days.

This caused them much grief, but they did not understand this word. It was hidden from them lest they should understand. And they were afraid to ask him about these words.

Section 86. THE MESSIAH PAYS THE TEMPLE TAX

Mark 9:33a.   Matthew 17:24-27

They arrived at Capernaum, and the collectors of the temple tax came to Peter and said, Your teacher pays the temple tax, does he not?

He answered, Yes.

When he came into the house, Jesus forestalled him, saying, What do you think, Simon? Whom do the kings of the earth receive taxes and tribute from, their own sons or aliens?

He said, From aliens.

Jesus said to him, Then the sons are free. However, lest we offend them, go and throw a hook into the sea and take the first fish which rises up. When you have opened his mouth, you will find a dollar.[5] Take that and pay them for you and me.

Section 87. Teachings on Childlikeness

Mark 9:33b-37.   Matthew 18:1-5.   Luke 9:46-48

In that hour his disciples came to him in the house and he asked them, What were you discussing along the way?

They kept still, for they had discussed with one another in the way as to who would be the greatest in the kingdom of heaven. However, Jesus knew the thoughts of their heart, so he sat down, called the twelve, and said to them, If anyone of you wishes to be first, he shall be the last of all and the servant of all.

Then he took a child and stood him before them. After he had taken him in his arms, he said, Truly, I tell you, except you turn and become as little children, you will certainly fail to enter the kingdom of heaven. Therefore, whoever will continue to humble himself as this child, he is the greatest in the kingdom of heaven. He who receives one of these children in my name receives me. He who receives me receives not me alone, but also him that sent me. He that is least among you all is great.

---

5. The Temple tax was a half-shekel. I have translated it "dollar" here to get an approximation of terms in American language.

Section 88. SERIES OF DISCOURSES ON OFFENDING AND FORGIVENESS

Jesus Rebukes the Intolerance of John

Mark 9:38-41.   Luke 9:49,50

John said to him, Master, we saw a man casting out demons in your name, but we forbade him because he did not follow us.

Jesus said to him, Stop forbidding him.   No one who does a mighty work in my name will be able to speak evil of me quickly. Whoever is not against us is for us.   Whoever gives you a cup of water in my name, because you are of the Messiah, I tell you truly that he will never lose his reward.

Jesus Teaches to Avoid Giving Offense

Mark 9:42-50.   Matthew 18:6-14

He that influences one of these little ones who believe in me to sin, it would be better for him to have a heavy millstone tied around his neck and be drowned in the deep sea.   Woe to the world because of things that cause sin!   It is necessary for such influences to come, but woe to the man through whom they come.   If your hand causes you to do sin, cut it off and throw if from you; it is better for you to enter life maimed than to be cast into the unquenchable fire of hell with both hands.   If your foot causes you to sin, cut it off and throw it from you; it is better for you to enter life lame than to be cast into hell with both feet.   If your eye causes you to sin, take it out and throw it from you; it is better for you to enter life with one eye than to be cast into hell fire where the worm does not die and the fire is never put out, having both eyes.   Surely, every one of you will be salted with fire.   Salt is good, but if the salt has become tasteless, how can it regain its power to season? Have salt in yourselves, and be at peace with one another.

See to it that you do not despise one of these little ones, for their angels are always in the presence of my Father which is in heaven. What do you think? If a man owns a hundred sheep and just one of them should stray away, will he not leave the ninety and nine upon the mountain and go seek the one which strayed? When he finds it, I tell you of a truth, he rejoices over it more than over the ninety and nine which never strayed. Likewise, it is not the wish of your Father in heaven that one of these least ones should perish.

Forgiveness of Our Brothers

Matthew 18:15-35

If your brother should sin, go and show him his fault between you and him alone. If he hears you, you have gained your brother. If he will not hear you, take one or two more with you, that in the mouth of two or three witnesses every word may be established. If he refuses to hear them tell it to the church. If he will not even listen to the church, let him be to you as a heathen and tax-collector. Truly, I say to you, whatever you bind on earth will have been bound in heaven, and whatever you release on earth will have been released in heaven.

Again, I tell you truly, if two of you shall agree on earth concerning anything that they shall ask it, it will be given to them by my Father who is in heaven. For where two or three are gathered together in my name, I am there in their midst.

Then Peter came and said, Lord, how many times must I forgive my brother if he sins against me? Seven times?

Jesus said to him, I do not tell you seven, but seventy times seven. Therefore the kingdom of heaven is to be compared to a certain king who wished to make a reckoning with his slaves. When he began to reckon, one was brought to him who owed ten million dollars. Since he did not have it to pay, the master ordered him to be sold, and his wife and children and all that he had to make payment. The slave fell down and worshipped him, saying, Have patience with me and I will pay you all. So the master took pity on that slave and released him, and even forgave the debt. However, the slave went out and found one of his fellow slaves who owed him twenty dollars. He took hold of his throat and said, Pay me what you owe. The fellow slave fell down and begged him, saying, have patience with me, and I will pay you. But he would not. He took him and threw him in prison till he should pay what he owed. His fellow slaves were filled with sorrow when they saw what happened, and they went and told the master of these things. His master called him and said, You are an evil slave. I forgave you all your debt because you begged me. Should not you have shown mercy also to your fellow slave just as I showed mercy to you? So his master was angry and delivered him to the torturers until he should pay everything which he owed. Thus also will my heavenly Father do to you if you do not each one forgive his brother from the heart.

Section 89. The Counsel of Jesus' Brothers

John 7:2-9

The Jewish Feast of the Tabernacles was near. His brothers therefore said to him, Come and go up to Judea, so that your disciples may see the works you are doing. No one does anything in secret if he seeks to be known openly. If you are going to do these things, show yourself publicly.

His brothers did not believe in him.

Jesus said to them, My time has not come yet, but your time is always at hand. The world cannot hate you, but it continues to hate me, for I continue to give testimony that its works are evil. Go on up to the feast. I am not going up to this feast, for my time is not fully completed.

He told them this and stayed on in Galilee.

Section 90. Jesus Goes Privately to Jerusalem
Through Samaria

Matthew 8:19-22.   Luke 9:51-52.   John 7:10

When his brothers had gone up to the feast, he also went up,
not publicly but as it were, secretly.   The days were soon to
be completed for him to be received up, so he set his face firmly
to go up to Jerusalem.   He sent messengers before him.   They
went on and entered into a village of the Samaritans to make
ready for him.   But they would not receive him because his
face was turned toward Jerusalem.   When James and John,
his disciples, saw it, they said, Lord do you want us to call
fire down from heaven and consume them?

He turned and rebuked them, then they went on to another
village.

As they went on in the way, a certain scribe[6] said to him,
Teacher I will follow you wherever you go.

Jesus said to him, The foxes have holes, and the birds of the
air have nests, but the Son of man does not even have a place
to lay his head.

Then he said to another disciple, Follow me.

He said, Let me go first and bury my father.

He said to him, Follow me.   Let the dead bury their own
dead: you go out and proclaim the kingdom of God.

Then still another man said, Lord, I will follow you, but first
let me say good-bye to those of my house.

Jesus said to him, No one who puts his hand to the plow and
keeps looking behind him is fit for the kingdom of God.

6. I have brought Matthew's record of this (Matthew 8:19-22) into chronological harmony with Luke's (9:51-62).   This is based both on the higher quality of Luke's chronology
and the more natural setting for the event as given by Luke.

CHAPTER XII

THE LATER JUDEAN MINISTRY[1]

Section 91. JESUS AT THE FEAST OF TABERNACLES

John 7:11-52

The Jews were seeking him at the feast and kept saying, Where is he? There was much murmuring about him among the people.

Some said, He is a good man.

Others said, No. He leads the people astray.

However, no one spoke openly of him for fear of the Jews.

When the feast was already half over, Jesus went up to the temple and began to teach. The Jews therefore were astonished, saying, How can this man who never went to school know the Scripture.

Jesus answered them, my teaching is not mine but his who sent me. If anyone wishes to do his will, he will know about the teaching, whether it is from God or whether I speak on my own authority. He that speaks on his own authority seeks his own glory; but he who seeks the glory of him that sent him is sincere, and there is no deceitfulness in him. Did not Moses give you the law? Yet, not one of you is keeping the law. Why do you seek to kill me?

The crowd answered, You have a demon. Who is seeking to kill you?

Jesus replied, I have done just one deed, and you are astonished. Moses gave you the ceremony of circumcision—not

---

1. The scene of this ministry is uncertain. It is recorded only by John and Luke. John gives those events which occurred in Jerusalem; there are no notes of place in Luke. Therefore, it is without absolute proof that one can say, "John gives the Jerusalem ministry and Luke that in the country of Judea" (Robertson, *Harmony*, p. 114). But since no other scene can be assigned to this ministry with certainty, and since Luke records in it a visit to Martha and Mary as if it took place naturally in his traveling from village to village, we may suppose that Judea is the scene of events recorded here.

that it had its origin with Moses but with the fathers—and you circumcize a man child even on the sabbath. Now if a man child receives this rite on the sabbath that the law of Moses might not be broken, why are you angry with me because I make a man fully whole on the sabbath? You ought not to judge by outward appearance, but by a righteous judgment.

Some of the people of Jerusalem said, This is the man whom they seek to kill, is it not? Lo, he speaks openly, and they say nothing to him. Can it be that the rulers know that he really is the Messiah? But we know where he came from; when the Messiah comes, no man will know where he is from.

Jesus cried out in the temple as he taught, You know me and know where I came from? I have not come from myself, but he that is true sent me, whom you do not know. I know him, because I am from him and he sent me.

So they tried to arrest him, but no one could so much as lay his hand on him, for his hour had not yet come. Many of the multitude believed in him and said, The Messiah, when he comes, cannot do greater signs than he does, can he?

The Pharisees heard the crowd whispering these things about him, so the chief priests and Pharisees sent officers to take him prisoner.

Jesus said, I am with you only a little while longer, then I go to him who sent me. You will seek me, but you will not find me. You will not be able to come where I am.

The Jews said to one another, Where is this man going that we cannot find him? Will he go to the Dispersion among the Greeks and teach the Greeks? What does he mean when he says, You will seek me, but you will not find me, and, You will not be able to come where I am.

On the last day, the great day of the feast, Jesus stood and cried out, If anyone is thirsty, let him come to me and drink. Whoever continues to believe in me will have, as the scripture promises, a river of living water flowing from within him.

This he said with reference to the Spirit which those who believe in him were going to receive. The Spirit was not given yet, since Jesus was not yet glorified.

Those in the crowd who had listened to these words, began to say, This truly is the Prophet? Others said, He is the Messiah. But some said, the Messiah will not come out of Galilee, will he? Does not the scripture say that the Messiah will come of the seed of David and from Bethlehem, the village where David lived? So there arose a division in the crowd about him. Some wanted to arrest him. But no man was able to lay his hands on him. Then the officers came back to the chief priests and Pharisees, and they asked, Why did you not bring him?

The officers answered, There never was a man who spoke like this man speaks.

The Pharisees replied, You are not deceived too, are you? None of the leaders of the Pharisees believe in him, do they? The people, because they do not know the law, are accursed.

Nicodemus said to them—he who had formerly gone to Jesus, being one of them—Our law does not judge a man before it hears from him and knows what he does, does it?

They answered him, Are you also from Galilee? Search, and you will see that no prophet arises from Galilee.

Section 92. Jesus Claims to Be the Light of the World[2]

John 8:12-59

After this, Jesus was speaking to them again, I am the light of the world. He who follows me will not walk in the darkness, but will have the light of life.

---

2. There is no certainty that all of this took place at the Feast of Tabernacles. Most harmonizers, however, place it together, and since there is no evidence to force a change, we have followed them. One paragraph—John 7:53 to 8:11—can no longer be regarded as a part of the text. The evidence is overwhelmingly against its inclusion.

The Pharisees said to him, You testify concerning yourself; your testimony is not true.

Jesus replied to them, Even if I testify concerning myself, my testimony is true, because I know where I came from and where I am going. But you do not know where I came from nor where I am going. You judge according to the flesh; I judge nothing. But if I judge, my judgment is true, for I am not alone, but he who sent me helps me   In your law it is written, The testimony of two men is true.   I testify of myself, and the Father who sent me testifies of me.

They said to him, Where is your Father?

Jesus answered, You know neither me nor my Father.   If you had known me, you would have known my Father also.

He spoke these words in the treasury as he taught in the temple, yet no one arrested him for his hour had not come.

He said to them again, I go away, and you will seek me and you will die in your sins.   Where I go, you cannot come.

The Jews began to say, Will he kill himself, that he says, You cannot come where I go?

He said to them, You are from below; I am from above. You are of this world; I am not of this world. Therefore, I said to you, You will die in your sins. For unless you believe that I am the Messiah, you will die in your sins.

They said to him, Who are you?

Jesus answered, Even what I have told you from the first. I still have many things to say and to judge about you. He that sent me is true, and the things which I now speak in the world are those things which I have heard from him.

They did not know that he spoke to them of the Father.

Jesus continued, When you have lifted up the Son of man, you will know that I am the Messiah. I do nothing of myself, but I am speaking these things just as the Father taught me. He who sent me is with me. He has not left me alone, for I always do what pleases him.

As he spoke these things, many believed in him.

Jesus said to the Jews who had believed on him, If you continue in my word, you will truly be my disciples; and you will know the truth, and the truth will set you free.

They answered, We are descendants of Abraham. We have never been in bondage to any man. How then do you say, You will be free?

Jesus answered them, I tell you of a truth that every man who practices sin is a slave to sin. The slave does not live in the house forever; the Son lives forever. If the Son shall set you free, you really will be free. I know that you are descendants of Abraham, but you are seeking to kill me because my word has no place in you. I speak the things which I have seen with my Father. You also are doing the things which you have heard from your father.

They answered, Abraham is our father.

Jesus said to them, If you were the sons of Abraham, you would practice the works of Abraham. But now you are seeking to kill me, a man who has spoken the truth to you which I heard from God. Abraham did not do this. You do the works of your father.

They said to him, We were not born in adultery. We have one father, God.

Jesus said to them, If God were you father, you would have loved me, for I came from God and am of God. I have not come by myself; he sent me. Why is it that you do not understand what I say? It is because you are not able to hear my word. You are of your father, the Devil, and the lusts of your father, you wish to practice. He was a murderer from the first, and has never stood in the truth, because truth is not in him. When he speaks a lie, he speaks of his own, for he is a liar and the father of lies. You do not believe me—one who speaks the truth. Who of you condemns me of sin? If I speak the truth, why do you not believe me? He who is of God hears the words of God. You do not hear, for you are not of God.

The Jews answered, Are we not right in saying, You are a Samaritan and have a demon?

Jesus replied, I have no demon; I honor my Father; you dishonor me. But I seek not my own glory; there is one who does seek it and judges. Truly, truly, I tell you that if any man keeps my word, he will never see death.

The Jews said to him, Now we know you have a demon. Abraham and the prophets died. Yet you say that if any man keeps your word, he will never taste death. You are not greater than our father Abraham who died, are you? The prophets also died. Whom do you make yourself?

Jesus answered, If I honor myself, my honor is nothing. My Father is the one who honors me, of whom you say, He is our God. You have not known him, but I know him. If I should say that I do not know him, I would be a liar like you. I know him, and I keep his word. Abraham your father rejoiced to see my day; and he saw and was glad.

The Jews said to him, You are not even fifty years old, and did Abraham see you?

Jesus said to them, I truly say to you, before Abraham came into existence, I AM.

Then they took up stones to stone him, but Jesus came out of the temple after hiding himself.

Section 93. JESUS HEALS A MAN BORN BLIND

John 9

As he went along, he saw a man who had been born blind. His disciples asked him, Rabbi, why was this man born blind? because of his own sin or that of his parents?

Jesus answered, Neither on account of his sin nor that of his parents, but that the works of God might be manifest in him. We must do the works of him that sent me while it is day; the night is coming when no man can work. While I am in the world, I am the light of the world.

This he said, then he spat on the ground and made clay out of the spittle; he put the spittle on his eyes and said to him, Go and wash in the pool of Siloam (which, being interpreted, is, Sent).

He went and washed and came, seeing.

His neighbors and those who had seen him before, for he had been a beggar, began to say, This is he who sat and begged, is it not?

Some said, It is he.

Others said, No, but he looks like him.

He said, I am he.

They said to him, How then were your eyes opened?

He replied, The man called Jesus made clay and anointed my eyes and said to me, Go to Siloam and wash. So I went and washed, and I have received my sight.

They said to him, Where is he?

He said, I do not know.

Then they brought the man who had been blind to the Pharisees. It was on the sabbath that Jesus had made clay and restored sight to his eyes. The Pharisees also asked him, How did you receive your sight?

He said to them, He put clay upon my eyes, and I washed, and I see.

Some of the Pharisees said, This man is not from God, for he does not keep the sabbath.

Others said, How can a sinner do such signs?

Thus a division arose among them. They said to the blind man again, What do you say about him who opened your eyes.

He said, He is a prophet.

But the Jews did not even believe that he had been blind and had received his sight until they called the parents of him who had received sight and asked them, Is this your son who you say was born blind? How then does he see now?

His parents answered, We know that he is our son and that he was born blind, but we do not know how it is that he sees now, nor do we know who restored his sight. Ask him. He is of age. He can speak for himself.

His parents said this because they were afraid of the Jews, for the Jews had already agreed to put anyone out of the synagogue who confessed Jesus. So his parents said, Ask him. He is of age.

They called the man who had been blind a second time and said to him, Give glory to God. We know this man is a sinner.

He answered, I do not know whether he is a sinner. One thing I do know: I was blind but now I see.

They said to him, What did he do to you? How did he restore your sight?

He replied, I have told you already, and you did not listen. Why do you want to hear it again? You do not wish to become his disciples, do you?

They began to abuse him and say, You are a disciple of that one; we are disciples of Moses. We know that God spoke to Moses; we do not even know where this man came from.

The man answered them, Why, this is a marvel. You do not know where he came from, yet he opened my eyes. We know that God does not hear sinners, but he hears anyone who worships God and lives to do his will. In all the ages it has not been heard that anyone opened the eyes of a man born blind. If this man were not from God, he would not be able to do anything.

They replied, You were completely born in sin, and do you think to teach us?

Then they cast him out.

Jesus heard that they had cast him out, so he found him and said, Do you believe in the Son of man?

He answered, Who is he, sir, that I may believe in him?

Jesus said to him, You have seen him, and he is talking to you now.

He said, Lord, I believe, and he worshipped him.

Jesus said, I have come into the world for judgment so that those who do not see may see, and those who see may become blind.

The Pharisees who were with him and heard these things said, We are not blind, are we?

Jesus said to them, If you were blind, you would have no sin. Now you say, We can see. Your sin remains.

Section 94. THE GOOD SHEPHERD

John 10:1-21

Truly, truly, I tell you, he that does not come in by the door into the sheepfold but climbs up some other way, that man is a thief and a robber. He that comes in through the door is the shepherd of the sheep. The door-keeper opens to him, and the sheep listen to his voice. He calls his own sheep by name and leads them out. When all of his own sheep are gone out, he goes before them, and the sheep follow him because they know his voice. They will not follow a stranger, but will flee from him, for they do not know the voice of strangers. This figure Jesus spoke to them, but they did not understand the meaning of his words.

Jesus said to them again, Truly, truly, I tell you, I am the door of the sheep. All who came before me are thieves and robbers, but the sheep did not listen to them. I am the door. If anyone comes in through me, he will be saved and will come in and go out and find pasture. The purpose of the thief is to steal and kill and destroy. I am come that they might have life and that they might have it abundantly. I am the good shepherd. The good shepherd lays down his life for the sheep. The hired man—he who is not even a shepherd, whose own the sheep are not—because he is a hired man and cares nothing for the sheep, sees the wolf coming and flees, leaving the sheep, and the wolf snatches and scatters them. I am the good shepherd. I know those who are mine, and they know me, just as the Father knows me and I know the Father. I lay down my life for the sheep. I have other sheep too, which are not of this fold. I must lead them also, and they will listen to my voice, and there will be one flock and one shepherd. Because I lay down my life and take it again, the Father loves me. No one takes it from me; I lay it down of myself. I have authority to lay it down, and I have authority to take it again, for I received this commandment from my Father.

A division arose among the Jews because of these words. Many were saying of him, He has a demon and is mad; why listen to him?

Others, however, said, These words do not come from a demon-possessed man. No demon can restore sight to the eyes of a blind man.

Section 95. The Seventy Go Out and Return

Matthew 11:20-30. Luke 10:1-24

After these things,[3] the Lord appointed seventy others and sent them on ahead of him by twos into every city and place

---

3. In this passage, Jesus pronounces woes upon the cities of Galilee which had rejected his message. Luke places this after his withdrawal from Galilee, at the beginning of his labors in a new field. Matthew places it in connection with the sending out of the twelve to labor in Galilee. Aside from the consideration of Luke's superior accuracy in matters of chronology, he has the more logical position for this material and is followed here.

where he himself was about to come. He said to them, The harvest truly is plentiful, but the workers are few. Pray the Lord of the harvest therefore to send out workers at once into his harvest. Go. Lo, I send you as lambs among wolves. Do not carry purse nor wallet nor sandals, and greet no one along the way. When you enter any house, first say, Peace to this house. If a son of peace is there, your peace will rest upon him. But if not, it will come back to you. Live in that house, eating and drinking what they provide, for the worker deserves his wages. Do not move from house to house. When you go into a city that welcomes you, eat the things set before you, heal the sick in it, and say to them, The kingdom of God has come near to you. But when you go into a city that rejects you, go at once into its streets and say, We are even wiping off the dust of your city, which has stuck to our feet, against you. Only keep on realizing that the kingdom of God has come near. I tell you, it will be easier for Sodom in that day than for that city.

Then he began to reproach those cities in which the most of his wonders had been done, because they had not repented. Woe to you, Chorazin! Woe to you, Bethsaida! for if the mighty deeds which were performed among you had been done in Tyre and Sidon, they would have repented long ago, sitting in sackcloth and ashes. Therefore, I tell you, it will be easier for Tyre and Sidon in the day of judgment than for you. And you, Capernaum, are you to be exalted to heaven? No, you will go down to hades. For if the mighty works which were performed in you had been done in Sodom, it would have remained to this day. I tell you, it will be easier for the land of Sodom in the day of judgment than for you.

Whoever listens to you listens to me; whoever rejects you rejects me. And whoever rejects me rejects him who sent me.

Then the seventy returned and said with joy, Lord, even the demons submitted to us in your name.

He said to them, I was looking when Satan fell from heaven like a flash of lightning. Lo, I have given you authority to tread on snakes and scorpions, and over all the power of the enemy, and nothing will ever harm you. However, stop rejoicing because the spirits are subject to you, but rejoice because your names have been enrolled in heaven.

In that very hour, he began to rejoice in the Holy Spirit, and he said, I make acknowledgment to thee, Father, Lord of heaven and earth, for you have hidden these things from the wise and learned and revealed them to babes. Yes, Father, for it was thy good pleasure to do this. All things have been intrusted to me by my Father, and no one knows the Son except the Father; nor does anyone know the Father except the Son, and he to whom the Son chooses to reveal him. Come to me, all of you who labor and are heavy laden; I will give you rest. Take my yoke upon you and learn from me, for I am gentle and humble of heart, and you will find rest for your souls. My yoke is easy and my burden is light.

Privately, he turned to his disciples and said, Blessed are the eyes that see what you see. I tell you that many prophets and kings have longed to see the things which you are seeng, but did not, and to hear the things which you are hearing, but did not.

Section 96. The Parable of the Good Samaritan

Luke 10:25-37

Lo, a lawyer stood up to tempt him by asking, Teacher, what shall I do to inherit eternal life?

He answered him, What is written in the law? How do you read it?

He answered, You shall love the Lord your God with all your heart, all your soul, all your strength, and all your mind; and your neighbor as yourself.

He said to him, You have answered correctly. Practice this and you will live.

But he, wishing to justify himself, said to Jesus, Who is my neighbor?

Jesus took him up and said, A man was going down from Jerusalem to Jericho, and he fell among robbers, who after stripping and beating him, went away, leaving him half-dead. It happened that a priest went down that way, but seeing him, he passed by on the other side. Likewise also a Levite, coming to the place and seeing him, passed by on the other side. But a Samaritan who was on a journey came to him, and when he saw him, he took pity on him. He came and bound up his wounds, pouring oil and wine on them. Then he put him on his own beast and brought him to an inn and took care of him. The next day he took out a half dollar and gave it to the inn-keeper, saying, Take care of him, and I will pay you whatever more it costs on my return. Which of these three do you think was a neighbor to him who fell among robbers?

He said, The one who took pity on him.

Jesus said to him, Go and practice the same thing.

Section 97. A Visit to Martha and Mary

Luke 10:38-42

While they were traveling along, he came to a certain village where a woman named Martha welcomed him to her house. She had a sister called Mary who took her seat at the Lord's feet and continued to listen to his words. But Martha became upset over so much serving. She broke in suddenly and said, Lord, do you not care that my sister is leaving me to serve alone? Tell her to help me.

The Lord replied, Martha, Martha, you are worried and wrought up over many things. But there is little needed, at most one dish. Mary has chosen the good portion, and it will not be taken from her.

Section 98. THE MODEL PRAYER

Luke 11:1-4

Once when he was praying in a certain place, his disciples came to him when he stopped and said, Lord, teach us to pray even as John taught his disciples.

He said to them, When you pray, say:

Father, may thy name be kept holy.
May thy kingdom come,
Give us day by day our daily bread,
And forgive us our sins,
For we have also forgiven everyone indebted to us.
Do not let us be overcome by temptation.

Section 99. PERSEVERANCE IN PRAYER

Luke 11:5-13

Then he said to them, suppose you have a friend, and you go to him in the middle of the night and say, Friend, lend me three loaves of bread, for a friend of mine has come to my house on a journey, and I have nothing to set before him.

But suppose he should reply, Stop troubling me; the door is already shut and my children are with me in bed; I cannot get up and give you anything.

I tell you, even if he will not get up and give to him because of friendship, yet because of his persistence he will get up and give him all he needs.

Therefore I tell you:

Keep asking, and it shall be given to you;
Keep seeking, and you shall find;
Keep knocking, and it shall be opened to you.
For everyone who keeps on asking receives;
He who keeps on seeking finds;
And to him who keeps on knocking it will be opened.

What father among you would give a stone to his son who is asking for bread? or if he asks for a fish, would give him a snake instead of a fish? or if he asks for an egg, would give him a scorpion? So if you who are evil know how to give good gifts to your children, how much more will your Father who is in heaven give the Holy Spirit to those who ask him?

Section 100. JESUS ANSWERS HIS ACCUSERS

Matthew 12:22-37, 43-45. Luke 11:14-28

A blind and dumb man who had a demon was brought to him.[4] He healed him. When the demon had gone out, the man could both see and speak. All the multitudes were filled with amazement and began to say, This one is not the Son of David, is he?

Some of them who were Pharisees said, He is casting out demons by the power of Beelzebub, the prince of demons. Others were seeking a sign from heaven of him to test him.

However, he knew their thoughts and said to them, Every kingdom which is divided against itself becomes desolate, and house falls upon house, and every city or house divided against itself must fall. If therefore Satan is divided against himself, how does his kingdom survive? Yet you say that I am casting out demons by the power of Beelzebub. Now if this is true, by whose power do your sons cast them out? They will be your judges. But if I cast out demons by the power of the Spirit of God, then the kingdom of God has come to you.

---

4. Both Luke and Mark have a similar account of the Beelzebub controversy, and the differences between them, as well as the usual chronological accuracy of each, argues for two such occurrences. It is entirely likely that the same accusation would be made against Jesus in both fields of labor and that similar answers would be given. Thus it is possible that such an event would occur during the Galilean campaign as Mark records, and also during the Perean campaign as Luke records. I have accepted the truth of two such events. The question is, Wihch one did Matthew record? The usual custom is to place his section in harmony with Mark and let Luke's account stand alone. But the affinities of language between Luke and Matthew in this account argue for a common source for their record other than Mark. Thus we assume that the source for their accounts is Q. Since Luke usually gives the correct order of this material, while Matthew very often arranges it topically, we have followed Luke's order and placed Matthew's account in harmony with his record.

When a fully armed, strong man guards his own premises, his property is secure. How can anyone enter the house of that strong man and seize his goods unless he first bind the strong man? However, when one stronger than he comes, he conquers him and strips him of the armor in which he trusted and distributes his spoil. He that is not with me is against me; he that gathers not with me scatters.

This is why I tell you that every kind of sin and blasphemy will be forgiven men, but the blasphemy of the Spirit will not be forgiven. Whoever speaks against the Son of man may receive forgiveness, but whoever speaks against the Holy Spirit will not receive forgiveness in this age nor the coming one.

When the unclean spirit goes out of a man, he passes through dry places trying to find a place to rest. When he fails to find it, he says, I will return to the house from which I came out. When he comes, he finds it unoccupied, swept clean, and in order. He then goes and brings seven other spirits more evil than himself, and entering in, they live there. The last condition of that man is worse than the first. Even so will it be to this wicked generation.

Either make the tree good and its fruit good, or else make the tree bad and its fruit bad, for the tree is known by its fruit. You brood of snakes, how can you speak good words when you are evil? Out of the abundance of the heart, the mouth speaks. The good man brings out good things from the good treasure, but the evil man brings out evil things from the evil treasure. I tell you that on the day of judgment men shall give an account of every careless word they speak. By your words you will be justified, and by your words you will be condemned.

Even while he was saying these things, a woman of the crowd lifted up her voice and said to him, Blessed is the mother who bore and nursed you.

He said, Yes, but better still, blessed are they who listen to the word of God and practice it.

Section 101. The Evil Generation

Matthew 12:38-42.   Luke 11:29-36

While the people continued to crowd around him, some of the scribes and Pharisees said, Master, we would like to see a sign from you.

He replied, This is an evil and adulterous generation.   It seeks a sign, but no sign will be given it except the sign of the prophet Jonah.   For as Jonah was three days and three nights in the whale's stomach, so will the Son of man be three days and three nights in the heart of the earth.   Jonah became a sign to the people of Nineveh; the Son of man will be the same to this generation.   The men of Nineveh will stand up in judgment with this generation and condemn it.   For they repented at the preaching of Jonah, and, lo, one greater than Jonah is here.   The queen of the South will stand up in judgment with the men of this generation and will condemn them.   For she came from the ends of the earth to hear the wisdom of Solomon, and, lo, one greater than Solomon is here.

No one lights a lamp and puts it in a cellar or under a measuring bucket, but he puts it on the lampstand so that those who enter may see the light.   Your eye is the lamp of your body.   When your eye is sound, the whole body is full of light.   When it is bad, your body is dark.   Be on your guard lest the light which is in you become darkness.   Therefore, if your whole body is full of light, having no part dark, it will all be illumined as when the lamp gives you light by its shining.

Section 102. The Pharisees Denounced for Hypocrisy

Luke 11:37-54

While he was speaking, a Pharisee invited him to eat with him.   He went in and reclined at the table.   The Pharisee was surprised when he saw that he did not wash before the meal. The Lord said to him, Now you Pharisees clean up the outside of the cup and plate, but inside you are full of greed and evil.

Fools! Did not he who made the outside make the inside too? Therefore, dedicate your inner self, and, lo, all things are clean to you.

Woe to you Pharisees! for you pay tithes on mint, rue, and every herb, but neglect justice and the love of God. You certainly ought to do these, though you should not neglect the other.

Woe to you Pharisees! for you love the chief seats in the synagogues and greetings in the market places.

Woe to you! for you are as unmarked graves which men walk over without knowing it.

One of the lawyers said to him, Teacher, when you say these things, you are also insulting us.

He said, Yes, woe to you lawyers also! for you put loads that are hard to carry on other men, but you yourselves do not touch the loads with one of your own fingers.

Woe to you! for you build tombs for the prophets whom your forefathers killed. Thus you testify that you approve the deeds of your forefathers, for they killed them and you build tombs for them. This is why the wisdom of God said, I will send prophets and apostles to them; some they will kill and some persecute; that the blood of all the prophets which has been continually shed from the foundation of the world may be required of this generation—from the blood of Abel to the blood of Zachariah, who perished between the altar and the sanctuary. Yes, I tell you that it will be required of this generation.

Woe to you lawyers! for you have taken away the key of knowledge, and though you will not enter in yourselves, you forbid those who try to enter.

When he had gone out, the scribes and Pharisees became greatly angered and began to ply him with more questions, lying in ambush to entrap him by what he said.

Section 103. WARNING AGAINST THE LEAVEN OF THE PHARISEES

Matthew 10:24-33.   Luke 12:1-12

Meanwhile, tens of thousands of people were coming together to him—so many that they walked on one another.

He began to say to his disciples first, The disciple is not above his teacher, nor the slave above his master.   It is enough for the disciple that he should be as his teacher, and the slave as his master.   If they have called the master of the house Beelzebub, how much more the members of his household! Beware of the leaven of the Pharisees—hypocrisy.   Do not fear them, for there is nothing covered which will not be uncovered, and nothing hidden which will not be known.   Tell in the light what I have spoken to you in the darkness.   Proclaim from the housetop what I have whispered in your ear.

I tell you, my friends, do not grow afraid of them who kill the body but are not able to kill the soul.   I will show you whom you should fear.   Fear him who has authority, after killing, to cast both soul and body into hell; yes, I tell you, fear him. Are not two sparrows sold for one cent and five for two cents? Yet, God forgets none of them; no, not even one shall fall to the ground without your Father.   Why, even the hairs of your head are numbered.   Stop being afraid!   You are of more value than many sparrows.

Everyone therefore who confesses to be in me before men, the Son of man will also confess to be in him before the Father and his angels in heaven.   But he that denies me before men, I will also deny him before my Father and his angels in heaven. So every one who speaks a word against the Son of man will be forgiven, but there is no forgiveness for him who blasphemes the Holy Spirit.

When they bring you before the synagogue or magistrates or authorities, do not worry about how you will defend yourselves or what you will say.   The Holy Spirit will teach you in that very hour what to say.

Section 104. The Rich Fool

Luke 12:13-21

Just then, a man in the crowd said to him, Teacher, tell my brother to divide the inheritance with me.

He said to him, Man, who has made me a judge or an umpire in your affairs.

Then to them all he said, Be on your guard against every kind of covetousness, for a man's life is not derived from his possessions even when he has an abundance.

He told them a parable: A certain rich man's farm produced well, so he reasoned with himself, saying, What shall I do? I have no place to store my crops.   Then he said, I will do this. I will pull down my barns and build larger ones, and I will store up all my grain and my goods there.   Then I will say to my soul, Soul, you have plenty of goods stored up for many years, take your ease; eat; drink; and enjoy life.   But God said to him, Fool, this night your soul will be demanded of you, and who will own these things that you have prepared?

So is every one who lays up treasure for himself and is not rich toward God.

Section 105. Faith in God's Care

Luke 12:22-34

He said to his disciples, Stop being anxious about your life, what you will eat; or for your body, what you will wear.   The life is more than food, and the body is more than clothing. Look at the ravens!   They neither sow nor reap, nor do they have barns and granaries to store up food.   Yet God feeds them. Are you not much more valuable than the birds?   Which of you being anxious can add one hour to his life?   If then you cannot do a very little thing, why are you anxious about the rest?   Consider how the lilies grow: they do not toil nor spin.

Yet, I tell you that even Solomon in all his splendor was not dressed like one of them. If God so clothes the grass which today is in the field but tomorrow is thrown into the oven, how much more will he clothe you, Oh you of little faith! Therefore, stop seeking what to eat or what to drink or what to wear, and stop living in suspense. All the people of the world continue to seek after these things. Your Father knows that you need them. So, you keep on seeking first his kingdom, and these things will be added to you.

Little flock, stop being afraid; your Father delights to give you the kingdom. Sell your possessions and give alms. Make purses for yourselves that do not grow old, a treasure unfailing in the heavens, where a thief cannot come near nor does a moth destroy it. For where your treasure is, there also your heart will be.

Section 106. WATCHFULNESS ENJOINED

Matthew 24:42-51. Luke 12:35-48

Keep your loins girded and your lamps burning; be like men who wait for the return of their master from the wedding feast, so they may open the door for him as soon as he comes and knocks. Happy are those servants whom the master finds watching when he comes. I tell you truly, he will gird himself, and make them recline at the table, and come to serve them. Whether he comes and finds them so in the second or in the third watch, happy are they.

Therefore, watch, for you do not know on what day your Lord may come. Be sure of this, if the master of the house had known in what watch the thief was coming, he would have watched and not allowed his house to be broken into. Be ready, therefore, for in such an hour as you least expect him, the Son of Man will come.

Peter said, Lord , do you speak this parable to us only or to all men?

The Lord said, Who then is that faithful and prudent steward whom the master has put in charge of his household to give out food in the proper time? Happy is that slave if the master finds him doing this when he comes. I tell you truly that he will put him in charge of all his property. But if that slave is evil and should say in his heart, My master delays his coming; and should begin to beat his fellow slaves, both men and women, and to eat and drink and be drunk, the master of that slave will come in a day when he is not expecting him and in an hour which he does not know. He will cut him in two and appoint him his portion among the unfaithful and hypocrites. There, the weeping and the gnashing of teeth will be. That slave who knows the will of his master, but does not make ready or do his will, will be beaten with many lashes. But he who does not know, though he does what is worthy of lashes, will be beaten with few. To whom much is given, much will be required of him; and to whom they entrust much, people will ask much more of him.

Section 107. THE MILITANT MISSION OF JESUS

Matthew 10:34-39. Luke 12:49-53

I have come to cast fire upon the earth; how I wish it were already kindled! I have a baptism to be baptized with; how I am urged on until its completion! Do you think that I have come to give peace to the earth? No, I tell you, I have not come to give peace, but a sword and divisions. From now on, five who dwell in a house will be divided; three against two and two against three. I have come to set father against son and son against father, mother against daughter and daughter against mother, mother-in-law against bride and bride against mother-in-law, and a man's own family will be his enemies.

He that loves his father or mother more than me is not worthy of me. He who loves son or daughter more than me is not worthy of me. He who does not take up his cross and follow after me is not worthy of me. He who saves his life will lose it, but he who loses his life for my sake will find it.

Section 108. The Signs of the Times

Luke 12:54-59

He began to say to the crowds, When you see a cloud rising in the west, you say at once, A rain is coming, and so it is. When a south wind blows, you say, It is a scorching wind, and it comes. You hypocrites, you know how to interpret the face of the earth and sky. Why can you not interpret this time? Why do you not judge the right for yourselves? As, for instance, when you go with your opponent before the magistrate, take pains to be rid of him on the way, lest he drag you before the judge, the judge deliver you to the officer, and the officer throw you into prison. I tell you, you will never come out of there until you have paid the last penny.

Section 109. The Necessity of Repentance

Luke 13:1-9

It was at this time that some people came to tell him about the Galileans whose blood Pilate had mingled with their sacrifices.

He said to them, Do you think, because they suffered so, that these Galileans were worse sinners than all Galileans? No, I tell you, but unless you repent, you will all likewise perish. Or those eighteen men who perished when the tower of Siloam fell on them, do you think they were worse offenders than all the people of Jerusalem? No, I tell you, but unless you repent, you will all perish in the same manner.

Then he told them this parable: A man had a fig tree planted in his vineyard, and when he came to pick its fruit, he found none. So he said to the vinedresser, Lo, I have come for three years seeking fruit on this fig tree and have found none; cut it down. Why does it waste the ground?

He replied, Master, leave it just for this year. Let me dig around it and throw manure on it, and it may bear fruit for the future; but, if not, you may cut it down.

Section 110. CRIPPLED WOMAN HEALED

Luke 13:10-17

He was teaching in one of the synagogues on the sabbath. And, lo, a woman was present who had had a spirit which caused infirmity for eighteen years; she was bent double and could not stand up straight at all. When Jesus saw her, he called to her, Woman you are free from your infirmity.

Then he laid his hands on her, and she straightened up instantly and began to glorify God.

The ruler of the synagogue was indignant because Jesus had healed on the sabbath, so he said to the crowd, There are six days on which work must be done. Come on them to be healed, not on the sabbath.

The Lord replied to him, Hypocrites, is it not true that each one of you unties his ox or his donkey and leads him to drink on the sabbath? Why should not this woman—a daughter of Abraham, and bound by Satan for eighteen years— be freed from this bondage on the sabbath day?

While he was saying these things, all who opposed him were blushing with shame, but all the people were rejoicing because of all the glorious things which had happened through him.

Section 111. JESUS REPEATS TWO PARABLES

Luke 13:18-21

He said, What is the kingdom of God like? To what shall I compare it? It is like a grain of mustard seed which a man took and threw into his garden. There, it grew and became a tree, and the birds of heaven took shelter in its branches.

Again he said, To what shall I compare the kingdom of God? It is like leaven which a woman took and hid in a bushel of flour until the whole of it was leavened.

Section 112. Teaching on the Way to Jerusalem

Luke 13:22-30

Then he began to go through the cities and villages, teaching as he made his way to Jerusalem.

A man said to him, Lord, are there only a few who will be saved?

He said to them, Keep on trying to enter through the narrow door; for many, I tell you, will try to come in and will not be able. Once the master of the house shall have arisen and closed the door, you may begin to stand outside and knock on the door, saying, Lord open to us. But he will answer, I do not know where you come from.

Then you will begin to say, We ate and drank before you, and you taught in our streets.

But he will say, I do not know where you come from; depart from me all you workers of iniquity.

There will be the weeping and the gnashing of teeth when you see Abraham, Isaac, Jacob, and all the prophets in the kingdom of God, and you yourselves cast out. Yes, they will come from the east and west and north and south and recline together in the kingdom of God. And, lo, those who are last will be first, and those who are first will be last.

Section 113. At the Feast of Dedication

John 10:22-39

Then was the Feast of Dedication in Jerusalem. It was winter, and Jesus walked in the temple on the porch of Solomon. The Jews therefore came around him and began to say to him, How long do you hold us in suspense? If you are the Messiah, tell us plainly.

Jesus answered them, I told you and you do not believe. The works which I do in the name of my Father testify of me.

GRADY DAVIS

You do not believe because you are not my sheep. My sheep hear my voice, and I know them, and they follow me. I give them eternal life, and they will never perish, Neither shall any man snatch them out of my hand. My Father who gave them to me is greater than all; no one is able to snatch them out of the Father's hand. I and the Father are one.

The Jews again took up stones to stone him.

Jesus answered them, Many good works have I showed you from my Father. For which of these do you stone me?

The Jews answered, We are not stoning you for a good work, but for blasphemy; for you, being only a man, make yourself God.

Jesus answered them, Is it not written in your law, I said you are gods? Now if they are called gods to whom the word of God came (and the scripture cannot be broken), why do you say that it is blasphemy for him whom God consecrated and sent into the world to say, I am the Son of God? If I am not doing the works of my Father, do not believe me. But if I do them, even though you do not believe me, believe the works, so that you may know and understand that the Father is in me, and I in the Father.

Therefore, they sought again to arrest him, but he escaped from their hands.

CHAPTER XIII

THE LATER PEREAN MINISTRY ?

Section 114. JESUS WITHDRAWS TO BETHANY BEYOND JORDAN

John 10:40-42

He went away again beyond Jordan to the place where John at first baptized, and lived there. Many came to him and said, John performed no sign, but all the things that he told us about this man are true. So many believed on him there.

Section 115. MESSAGE TO HEROD AND LAMENT OVER JERUSALEM

Luke 13:31-35

In that hour, some Pharisees came and said to him, Rise up and get away from here, for Herod wants to kill you.

He said to them, Go and tell that fox, Lo, I cast out demons and perform cures today and tomorrow, and on the third day I will complete my work. But I must go on my way today and tomorrow and the next day, for it is impossible for a prophet to perish outside Jerusalem.

O Jerusalem, Jerusalem, you who kill the prophets and stone those sent to you! How often have I longed to gather your children to me as a hen gathers her young under her wing, but you refused. Lo, your house is left to you. I tell you, you will not see me until you say, Blessed is he who comes in the name of the Lord.

Section 116. JESUS AT A PHARISEE'S FEAST

Luke 14:1-24

One Sabbath day when he went into the house of one of ruling Pharisees to eat bread, they were watching him closely. And lo, there was a man in front of him who suffered from dropsy. Jesus said to the lawyers and Pharisees, Is it lawful to heal on the sabbath or not?

They made no answer. So he took hold of the man and healed him and sent him away. Then he said to them, Which of you, if your son or your ox should fall into a well, will not pull him up at once on the sabbath day?

They could make no reply to these things.

He spoke a parable to those who reclined at the table—he had noticed that they chose the first seats—saying, When you are invited by anyone to a wedding feast, do not recline in the chief seat. If you do, someone more honorable than you may have been invited, and he who invited you both may come and say to you, Give this man your place. Then you will begin to take the lowest place with shame. But when you are invited, go and recline at the lowest place, so that when he who invited you shall come, he will say to you, Friend, come up higher. Then you will be honored before all your fellow guests. For everyone who exalts himself will be humbled, but he who humbles himself will be exalted.

He said to the man who had invited him, When you make a luncheon or dinner, stop inviting your friends and your brothers and your relatives and your rich neighbors. If you do, they may invite you in return, and you will be repaid. But when you give a feast, invite the poor, the crippled, the lame, and the blind. Then you will be blessed, for they have nothing to repay you, but you will be repaid at the resurrection of the just.

When one of the fellow guests heard these things, he said to him, Blessed is the man who eats bread in the kingdom of God.

He said to him, A certain man was having a great dinner, and he invited many. When the hour of the dinner arrived, he sent a slave to those whom he had invited to say, Come on now for all things are ready.

But they all with one voice began to make excuse.

The first said to him, I have bought a field and must go and look at it. I ask you to excuse me.

Another said, I have bought five yoke of oxen and go to try them out. I ask you to excuse me.

Still another said, I have married a wife. Therefore, I cannot come.

The slave returned and reported these answers to his master. The master of the house was angered and said to his slave, Go out immediately into the streets and lanes of the city and bring in here the poor, the crippled, the blind, and the lame.

The slave said, Master, what you ordered is done, and there is still room.

The master said to his slave, Go out into the highways and the hedgerows and compel them to come in that my house may be filled. I tell you, not one of those men who were invited shall even taste my dinner.

Section 117. COUNTING THE COST OF DISCIPLESHIP

Luke 14:25-35

Great crowds were going along with him. Turning to them, he said, If any one comes to me and does not hate his father and mother and wife and children and brothers and sisters, yes, and even his own life, he cannot be my disciple. Whoever does not continue to bear his cross and come after me cannot be my disciple.

Who of you, when you wish to build a tower, does not first sit down and calculate the cost to see if he has enough to complete it? If he does not, he may get the foundation laid and be unable to complete it, and all those who see it will begin to mock him, saying, This man began to build and cannot finish it.

Or what king, when he is going to fight a battle with another king, does not first sit down and deliberate whether he is able with ten thousand to meet him who comes against him with twenty thousand? If not, he sends a delegation to ask for peace while the other is still far from him.

So then, everyone of you who does not renounce all his own belongings cannot be my disciple. Salt is good, but if even the salt becomes tasteless, how shall it regain its power to season? It is fit for neither soil nor manure. Men throw it away. He that has ears to hear, let him hear.

Section 118. God's Care for the Lost

Luke 15:1-32

All the tax-collectors and sinners kept drawing near to hear him. So the Pharisees and scribes kept grumbling, saying, This man welcomes sinners and eats with them.

The Lost Sheep

He told them this parable: What man among you if he has a hundred sheep and loses one of them, will not leave the ninety-nine in the desert and go after the lost one until he finds it? And having found it, he will place it on his shoulder, rejoicing. When he comes to his house, he calls in his friends and neighbors, saying to them, Rejoice with me for I have found my sheep which was lost.

I tell you that in the same way there will be more joy in heaven over one sinner who repents than over ninety-nine upright men who need no repentance.

The Lost Coin

Or, what woman, if she has ten coins and loses one, will not light a lamp and sweep the house and keep on seeking carefully until she finds it? When she has found it, she will call her friends and neighbors together, saying, Rejoice with me, for I have found the coin which was lost. Likewise, I tell you, there will be joy before the angels of God over one sinner that repents.

The Lost Son

Then he said, A man had two sons. The younger of them said to his father, Father, give me the share of the property which falls to me.

So he divided the property between them. Soon afterward, the younger son gathered all things together and went into a far country. There, he squandered his property in prodigal living. When he had spent it all, there came a great famine in that country, and he began to be in need. He went and united himself to one of the citizens of that country, and he sent him into his fields to feed hogs. Often he wanted to eat the carob pods which the hogs ate. But no one gave to him.

Then he came to himself and said, How many of my father's hired servants have more food than they can eat, while I am here dying of hunger. I will rise up and go to my father and I will say to him, Father, I have sinned against heaven and before you. I no longer deserve to be called your son. Make me as one of your hired servants.

So he arose and came to his own father. While he was still coming from afar, his father saw him and took pity on him, and he ran and embraced him and kissed him eagerly.

His son said to him, Father, I have sinned against heaven and before you. I no longer deserve to be called your son.

But the father said to his slaves, Quick, bring a robe, the finest one, and put it on him, and give him a ring for his hands and sandals for his feet, and bring the fatted calf; slay it, and let us eat and be merry. This, my son, was dead and is alive again, was lost and is found.

So they began to make merry.

The older son was in the field. As he came near to the house, he heard music and dancing. He called one of the servant boys and asked what this meant.

He said to him, Your brother has come, and your father killed the fatted calf because he received him back safely.

He became angry and would not go in.

Then his father came out and began to plead with him.

But he answered his father, Lo all these years I have served you and never disobeyed one of your commands. You have never even given me a kid that I might make merry with my friends. But when this son of yours who consumed your goods with harlots came, you killed the fatted calf for him.

He said to him, Son, you are always with me and all I have is yours. But it was our duty to make merry and rejoice, for this, your brother, was dead and now lives; he was lost and now he is found.

Section 119. The Parable of the Dishonest Steward

Luke 16:1-13

He continued speaking to the disciples, There was a rich man who had a steward, and he was accused to him of squandering his property. So he called him and said, What is this that I hear about you? Give an account of your stewardship; you can no longer be a steward.

The steward said to himself, What shall I do now that my master is taking the stewardship from me? I am not able to dig; I am ashamed to beg. I know what I will do to make sure that they will receive me into their homes when I am removed from the stewardship.

So he called each one of his master's debtors and said to the first one, How much do you owe my master?

He said, Nine hundred gallons of oil.

He said to him, Take your bill and sit down right away and write on it four hundred and fifty.

He said to another, How much do you owe?

He said, A thousand bushels of wheat.

He said to him, Take your bill and write eight hundred.

Well, the master of the dishonest steward praised him for acting shrewdly. The sons of this world are more shrewd toward their own generation than the sons of light. I tell you, use mammon, though it is tainted, to make friends for yourselves so that when it fails, they will welcome you into the eternal tabernacles. He that is faithful in the smallest things is faithful also in much, and he that is dishonest in the smallest thing is dishonest in much. Therefore, if you do not prove faithful in the use of evil mammon, who will trust you with true riches? And if you do not prove faithful with what is another's, who will give you what is ours?[1] No slave can serve two masters: he will hate one and love the other, or else he will be loyal to one and despise the other. You cannot serve God and mammon.

Section 120. The Rich Man and Lazarus

Luke 16:14-31

The Pharisees had heard all these things and, being lovers of money, they scoffed at him.

He said to them, You are those who justify yourselves in the sight of men, but God knows your hearts. For what is prized among men is an abomination before God. The law and the prophets were until John. Since then, the kingdom of God is preached and everyone is pressing into it. It is easier for heaven and earth to pass away than for one letter of the law to lapse. Everyone who leaves his wife and marries another commits adultery, and he who marries the divorced woman commits adultery.

---

1. The textual evidence is in favor of this reading, though its meaning is obscure "Ours" may refer to "true riches," thus referring to what Christ is to give.

Once there was a rich man who wore purple and fine linen and made merry every day with great display. A certain beggar, named Lazarus, who was covered with sores, was laid at his gate hoping to be filled by what fell from the rich man's table. Why, even the dogs used to come and lick his sores. One day the beggar died and was carried away by the angels to the bosom of Abraham. The rich man died and was buried. In Hades, he lifted up his eyes, being in agony, and saw Abraham afar off and Lazarus in his bosom.

He called out, Father Abraham, take pity on me and send Lazarus to dip the tip of his finger in water and cool my tongue, for I am in anguish in this flame.

Abraham replied, Son, remember that you received your good things during your life, just as Lazarus received evil. Now he is being consoled here, but you are in anguish. Besides, in all these regions, a great chasm remains fixed between us and you. Those who might want to go from here to you cannot, nor can they come from there to us.

He said, I beg you then, Father, to send him to my father's house, for I have five brothers, that he may warn them, lest they also should come to this place of torment.

Abraham replied, They have Moses and the prophets. Let them hear them.

He said, No, father Abraham, but if someone went to them from the dead, they would repent.

He answered, If they will not hear Moses and the prophets, neither would they be persuaded even if someone should rise from the dead.

Section 121. OFFENSES, FAITH, FORGIVENESS

Luke 17: 1-10

He said to his disciples, It is inevitable that snares to sin will come, but woe to him through whom they come! It would be better for him to be thrown into the sea with a millstone tied around his neck than for him to cause one of these little ones to sin.

Watch each other. If your brother sins, rebuke him; and if he repents, forgive him. Even if he sins against you seven times in one day; and seven times turns and says, I repent, forgive him.

The apostles said to the Lord, Add faith to us.

The Lord said to them, If you have faith as a grain of mustard, you might have said to this mulberry tree, Be rooted up and be planted in the sea, and it would have obeyed you.

Which of you will say to this slave, who has been ploughing in the field or tending sheep, when he comes in, Come now and recline at the table? Will he not rather say, Prepare my meal; gird yourself and serve me while I eat and drink, and after that you may eat and drink? Does he feel gratitude toward the slave because he did what he was told? Likewise you, when you have done all the things you were told to do, say, We are unprofitable slaves; we have done only what we ought to have done.

Section 122. THE RAISING OF LAZARUS

John 11:1-44

A certain man was sick, Lazarus of Bethany, the village of Mary and her sister Martha. Mary was the one who anointed the Lord with perfume and wiped his feet with her hair, whose brother Lazarus was sick.

The sisters sent to him and said, Lord, lo, the one you love is sick.

When Jesus heard it, he said, This sickness is not unto death but for the glory of God, that the Son of God may be glorified through it.

Jesus loved Martha and her sister and Lazarus. When he heard that he was sick, however, he stayed on in that place for two days. After this he said to the disciples, Let us go back to Judea.

The disciples began to protest, Rabbi, the Jews already are seeking to stone you, will you go back there?

Jesus answered, Are there not twelve hours in a day? If anyone goes walking in the daytime, he does not stumble, for he sees the light of this world. But if anyone goes walking in the night time, he stumbles, for the light is not in him.

This he said, and afterward he added to them, Our friend Lazarus is sleeping, but I am going to awaken him.

The disciples said to him, Lord, if he is sleeping he will recover.

Now Jesus had spoken about his death. However, they thought that he spoke of taking rest by sleep. So Jesus told them plainly, Lazarus has died. But I am glad for your sake that I was not there, that you may be led to believe. Let us go to him.

Thomas, the twin, said to his fellow disciples, Let us also go that we may die with him.

When Jesus came, he found that he had already been in the tomb for four days. Bethany was near to Jerusalem, about two miles away. Many of the Jews had come to Martha and Mary to console them concerning their brother. When Martha heard that Jesus was approaching, she went to meet him, but Mary stayed on in the house.

Martha said to Jesus, Lord, if you had been here, my brother would not have died. But even now I know that whatever you ask God, God will give you.

Jesus said to her, Your brother will rise again.

Martha said to him, I know that he will rise in the last day at the resurrection.

Jesus said to her, I am the resurrection and the life.   He who believes in me, even if he has died, will live; and everyone who lives and believes in me shall never die.   Do you believe this?

She said to him, Yes, Lord, I have come to believe that you are the Messiah, the Son of God, the one who comes into the world.

On saying this, she went and called her sister, Mary, and said quietly, The teacher has come and is calling for you.

As soon as she heard it, she jumped up and started to him, for Jesus had not yet come into the village but was still in the place where Martha had met him. The Jews who were with her in the house, consoling her, saw Mary jump up and go out, and they followed her, thinking that she was going out to the tomb to weep there.

As Mary came up to Jesus and saw him, she fell at his feet, saying to him, Lord, if you had been here, my brother would not have died.

Jesus saw her weeping and the Jews who had come with her weeping, and he began to groan in his spirit and be troubled within himself, and he asked, Where have you laid him?

They answered, Lord, come and see.

Jesus began to weep.

The Jews therefore said, See how he loved him.

But some of them said, Would not this man who can open the eyes of the blind have been able to prevent his death?

Jesus groaned again within himself as he came to the tomb. It was a cave, and a stone had been placed over it.

Jesus said, Take the stone away.

Martha, the sister of the dead man, said, Lord, he will stink by now, for it is four days since he died.

Jesus said to her, Did I not tell you that if you will only believe, you will see the glory of God?

Then they took the stone away.

Jesus lifted up his eyes and said, Father, I thank thee that thou hast heard me. I have known all along that thou didst hear me. But for the sake of the crowd which stands around, I said it, that they may believe that thou didst send me.

On saying this, he called out in a loud voice, Lazarus, come out!

The dead man came out, bound hand and foot with bandages, and a napkin tied around his face.

Jesus said to them, Untie him and let him go.

Section 123. THE EFFECTS OF RAISING LAZARUS

John 11:45-54

Many of the Jews therefore who had come with Mary saw what he did and believed in him. But some of them went to the Pharisees and reported what Jesus had done. Therefore, the chief priests and the Pharisees called a council and said, What shall we do? for this man is doing many signs. If we let him keep on doing this, all men will believe in him, and the Romans will come and take away our place and our nation.

One of them, Caiaphas, who was high priest that year, said to them, You know nothing; neither do you take into account that it is to your advantage for one man to die for the people, and not that the whole nation be destroyed.

This he said, not from himself, but because he was high priest that year, he prophesied that Jesus was going to die for the nation; and not for the nation only, but also that he might gather into one the children of God who are scattered abroad.

From that day therefore they were seeking to put him to death. This was why Jesus no longer walked openly in Judea but went away into the country near the desert, to a city called Ephraim, and he stayed there with his disciples.

Section 124. THE TEN LEPERS AND DISCOURSE ON THE LAST DAYS

Luke 17:11-37

As Jesus was going to Jerusalem, he passed through Samaria and Galilee. When he entered one of the villages, ten lepers met him. They stood at some distance and lifted their voices, saying, Jesus, Master, take pity on us.

When he saw them, he said, Go show yourselves to the priests.

While they were going, they were cleansed.

One of them, seeing that he was cured, turned back and glorified God with a great voice, and he fell down upon his face at his feet, thanking him. He was a Samaritan.

Jesus said, Were not ten cleansed? Where then are the nine? Is no one found to turn back and give glory to God except this foreigner.

Then he said to him, Rise up; go your way. Your faith has made you well.

When he was questioned by the Pharisees as to when the kingdom of God would come, he answered them, The kingdom of God comes not with outward display; neither do men say, Lo, here or there. For, you see, the kingdom of God is within you.

He said to the disciples, The time will come when you will long to see one of the days of the Son of man, but you will not

see it. They will say to you, Lo, there; lo, here. Be not led
astray, neither run after them. For just as the lightning shines
from one horizon to the other when it flashes, so will the Son
of man be in his day. But first he must suffer many things
and be rejected by this generation. Just as it was in the days
of Noah, so will it be also in the days of the Son of man. They
were eating, drinking, marrying, and giving in marriage until
the day when Noah entered the ark; then the flood came and
destroyed them all. It happened just the same way in the
days of Lot. They were eating, drinking, buying, selling,
planting, and building. But on the day when Lot came out
of Sodom, fire and brimstone rained down from heaven and
destroyed them all. It will be just the same way in the day
when the Son of man is revealed. On that day, if one should
be on the housetop and his goods in the house, let him not come
down to take them. Likewise, if one is in the field, let him not
turn back. Remember Lot's wife. Whoever seeks to use his
life for himself will lose it, but whoever loses it will save it. I
tell you, on that night, two men will be in one bed; one will be
taken and the other left. Two women will be grinding upon
the same mill; one will be taken and the other left.

They answered him, Where, Lord?

He said to them, Where the body is, there also will the
vultures be gathered together.

Section 125. Two Parables on Prayer

Luke 18:1-14

He spoke a parable to them to show the necessity of praying
at all times and never giving up, saying, In a certain city there
was a judge who had no fear for God nor respect for man.
There was also a widow in that city who kept coming to him,
saying, Give me justice against my adversary.

He would not for a time. Afterward, however, he said to
himself, Though I do not fear God nor respect man, yet because

this widow keeps bothering me, I will give her justice, lest she keep on coming and harassing me to the end.

Then the Lord said, You hear what the unrighteous judge says. Will not God surely give justice to his elect who call upon him day and night? I tell you, he will quickly give them justice. But still, when the Son of man comes, will he find faith upon the earth?

To some who had confidence in themselves that they were upright and scorned all the rest, he spoke this parable: Two men went up to the temple to pray, one a Pharisee, the other a tax-collector.

The Pharisee stood and prayed thus to himself, Oh God, I thank thee that I am not like the rest of men—robbers, rogues, adulterers—or even like this tax-collector. I fast twice each week. I give tithes of all that I gain.

But the tax-collector stood afar off and would not even lift his eyes to heaven, but beat on his breast continually, saying, Oh God, have mercy on me, the sinner.

I tell you, this man rather than the other went down to his house justified. For everyone who exalts himself will be humbled, and he who humbles himself will be exalted.

Section 126. Jesus Teaches Concerning Divorce

Mark 10:1-12.   Matthew 19:1-12

When Jesus had finished these words, he rose up and left Galilee and came into that part of Judea which is beyond Jordan. There great multitudes came together to him, and, as his custom was, he taught and healed them.

Some Pharisees came to him, and to tempt him, they said, Is it lawful for a man to divorce his wife for every cause?

He said to them, What did Moses command you?

They said, Moses permitted us to write a bill of divorce and divorce her.

Jesus said to them, Because of the hardness of your hearts, he wrote this commandment. But it was not so from the beginning. Have you never read that he who made them, made them male and female from the beginning, and said, For this reason a man shall leave his father and mother and be joined to his wife, and the two shall become one flesh? Thus they will not be two any longer, but one flesh. What therefore God has joined together, let man stop separating.

On reaching the house, the disciples asked him again about this. He said to them, I tell you that whoever divorces his wife except for fornication and marries another commits adultery, and if a woman should divorce her husband and marry another, she commits adultery.

The disciples were saying, If this is the case between a man and his wife, it is not best to marry.

He replied, Not every man can receive this saying, only those to whom it is granted. There are eunuchs which were so from birth, and there are eunuchs who are made such by men, and there are eunuchs who make themselves eunuchs for the sake of the kingdom of heaven. He that is able to receive it, let him receive it.

Section 127. JESUS BLESSES THE LITTLE CHILDREN

Mark 10:13-16. Matthew 19:13-15. Luke 18:15-17

They brought little children to him that he might lay his hands on them and pray. But the disciples, when they saw it, rebuked them.

When Jesus saw this, he was indignant and said to them, Let the little children come to me; stop hindering them; for of such as these is the kingdom of God. Truly, I tell you, whoever does not receive the kingdom of God as a little child will certainly not enter into it. Then he took them in his arms, and laying his hands on them, he blessed them. After that, he went away.

Section 128. THE RICH YOUNG RULER

Mark 10:17-31.   Matthew 19:16 to 20:16.   Luke 18:18-30

As he was going on his way, a ruler ran up and kneeled before him, asking, Good teacher, what good deed must I do to inherit eternal life?

Jesus said to him, Why do you call me good? No one is good except God. If you really want to enter into life, keep the commandments.

He said, Which?

Jesus said, Do not kill; do not commit adultery; do not steal; do not bear false witness; do not defraud; honor your father and mother; and love your neighbor as yourself.

The young man replied, Teacher, I have kept all these from childhood. What do I lack now?

Having heard, Jesus looked on him and loved him and said, If you want to be perfect, go sell what you have and give it to the poor, and you will have treasure in heaven. Then come, follow me.

When he heard this, he became greatly grieved and went away in distress, for he had many possessions.

The Hindrance of Riches

Jesus looked around and said to his disciples, I tell you of a truth, it is with great difficulty that those who are rich enter the kingdom of God.

The disciples were surprised at his words

Jesus added, Children, how difficult it is to enter the kingdom of God. I tell you of a truth, it is easier for a camel to go through the eye of a needle than for a rich man to enter the kingdom of God.

They were exceedingly amazed and said, Who then can be saved?

Jesus looked on them and said, With men this is impossible, but with God all things are possible.

Rewards of the Kingdom

Peter began to say to him, See! we have left all things and followed you. What will our reward be?

Jesus answered them, Truly, I tell you, in the restoration, when the Son of man shall sit on his throne of glory, you who have followed me will also sit on twelve thrones, judging the twelve tribes of Israel. There is no man who has left house or wife or brothers or sisters or mother or father or children or fields for my name's sake and for the sake of the gospel but will receive a hundredfold now in this time of houses and brothers and sisters and mothers and children and fields with persecution, and in the coming age life eternal. But many who are now first will be last, and the last will be first.

The Parable of the Laborers

For the kingdom of heaven is like a householder who went out early in the morning to hire laborers for his vineyard. When he had agreed with the workers for twenty cents a day, he sent them into his vineyard. He went out again at nine o'clock and saw some others standing idle in the market place. To them he said, Go also into the vineyard, and I will pay you what is right. And they went. He went out again at noon and at three o'clock and did the same thing. About five o'clock he went out and found others standing, and he said to them, Why do you stand here idle the whole day?

They answered him, Because no man hired us.

He said to them, Go also into the vineyard.

When evening came, the master of the vineyard said to the steward, Call the workers and pay them their wages, beginning with the last and ending with the first.

When those came who were hired at five o'clock, they received twenty cents.

Then those came who were hired first, and they supposed that they would receive more, but they also received twenty cents. As they took it, they began to grumble against the householder, saying, These last worked only one hour and you have made them equal to us who have borne the burden of the day and worked in the heat.

He answered them, Friend, I do you no wrong. Did you not agree with me for twenty cents? Take it and go. If I want to give this last man as much as you, have I not the right to do what I wish with my own? Or are you envious because I am generous?

So the last will be first, and the first last.

Section 129. PREDICTION OF DEATH AND REBUKE OF AMBITION

Mark 10:32-45. Matthew 20:17-28. Luke 18:31-34

They were on the way, going up to Jerusalem, and Jesus was going on before them. They were amazed and those who followed were afraid. Calling the twelve apart, he began to tell them the things which were about to happen to him, Listen! we are going up to Jerusalem, and all the things which were written by the prophets about the Son of man will be fulfilled. He will be delivered to the chief priests and scribes, and they will condemn him to death. They will deliver him to the Gentiles to be mocked and insulted and spit upon and scourged and put to death. But after three days, he will rise again.

They understood none of these things; yes, this word was hidden from them, so they did not know what he was talking about.

At that time, the mother of James and John, the sons of Zebedee, came and knelt before him with her sons and said, Master, we want you to grant us a request.

He said, What is your request?

She said to him, Grant that these, my two sons, may sit, one on your right hand and the other on your left hand in your kingdom and in your glory.

Jesus said to them, You do not realize what you are asking. Are you able to drink the cup I am about to drink and be baptized with the baptism that I am to be baptized with?

They said to him, We are able.

Jesus said to them, You will indeed drink the cup that I drink and be baptized with the baptism with which I am baptized. But to sit on my right hand and on my left is not mine to grant; it will be given to those for whom it has been prepared by my Father.

When the ten heard it, they began to be indignant with James and John.

Jesus called them to him and said, You know that those who seem to rule the Gentiles lord it over them, and their great men exercise authority over them. It shall not be like this among you. Whoever desires to become great among you, he shall be your servant; and whoever desires to become chief among you, he shall be the slave of all. For even the Son of man came not to be served, but to serve and to give his life a ransom for many.

Section 130. TWO BLIND MEN HEALED NEAR JERICHO

Mark 10:46-52.   Matthew 20:29-34.   Luke 18:35-43

They came to Jericho. As he was leaving (old) Jericho with his disciples and a great crowd, and as he approached (new)

Jericho, lo, two blind beggars sat beside the road begging.[2] One of them was Bartimaeus, the son of Timaeus. When they heard the crowd passing by, they inquired what this might be. They told them, Jesus of Nazareth is passing by.

When they heard that it was Jesus of Nazareth, they began to cry aloud, Jesus, you Son of David, take pity on us.

Many of the crowd began to tell them to be quiet. But they only cried out the louder, Master, Son of David, take pity on us.

Jesus stood still and told them, Tell them to come here.

So they called the blind men and said to them, Take courage rise up; he calls for you.

They threw off their garments and leaped up and came to Jesus. As they came near, he asked them, What is it that you want me to do for you.

They said, Master, open our eyes that we may receive our sight again.

His heart being moved with pity, Jesus touched their eyes and said, Receive your sight. Go. Your faith has made you whole.

Immediately, they received their sight and followed him, glorifying God. So all the people, seeing, gave praise to God.

Section 131. ZACCHEUS THE TAX-COLLECTOR

Luke 19:1-10

He entered Jericho and began to pass on through it. Lo, there was a rich man there named Zaccheus who was chief of tax-collectors. He was trying to see who Jesus was, but he

2. A. T. Robertson, *A Harmony of the Gospels* (Nashville, Tenn.: Sunday School Board, 1922), p. 149: "Matthew mentions two blind men, while Mark and Luke describe one, probably the more conspicuous one.—The discrepancy as to place, 'as he went out from Jericho,' "as he drew nigh unto Jericho," is best explained by the recent suggestion that the healing occurred after he left the old Jericho and as he was approaching the new Jericho which Herod the Great had built at some distance away."

could not because of the crowd, since he was small of stature. So he ran on ahead and climbed up into a fig mulberry tree so he could see him, for he was going to pass that way. When he came to the place, Jesus looked up and said to him, Zaccheus, come down at once; I must stop at your house today.

He quickly came down and welcomed him joyfully.

When they all saw it, they began to murmur, saying, He has gone to lodge with a sinner.

Zaccheus stood up and said to the Lord, Lo, I will give half of my property to the poor; and if I have robbed any man of anything, I will pay him back four times as much.

Jesus said to him, Today has salvation come to this house, seeing that even this man is a son of Abraham. For the Son of man has come to seek and to save the lost.

Section 132. The Parable of the Pounds
Luke 19:11-28

While they were listening to this, he added a parable because he was near to Jerusalem and some thought the kingdom of God was about to be openly manifested.

He said, A nobleman went to a far country to receive a kingdom for himself and then return. He called ten of his slaves and gave each twenty dollars. He said to them, Do business with this until I return.

His citizens kept on hating him and sent a delegation after him, saying, We do not want this man to rule over us. Upon his return, after he had obtained his kingdom, he summoned these slaves to him, to whom he had given the money, to learn what business they had done.

The first came, saying, Master your twenty dollars has earned ten times as much.

He said to him, Well done, good slave! you have proved faithful in a little; rule over ten cities.

The second came, saying, Your twenty dollars, master, has earned five times as much.

He said to him, You also rule over five cities.

The other one came and said, Master, here is your twenty dollars which I kept laid away in a napkin. I was afraid of you, for you are a stern man. You take up what you did not put down; you reap what you did not sow.

He said to him, I will judge you by your own words, wicked slave. You knew that I am a stern man, taking up what I did not put down and reaping what I did not sow, did you? Why then did you not put my money in the bank? Then, when I came, I would have received it with interest.

To those standing around, he said, Take the twenty dollars away from him and give it to the man who has two hundred.

They said, Master, he has two hundred already.

I tell you, that to everyone who acquires it will be given, and from him who does not acquire, even what he has will be taken away. And these enemies of mine who do not want me to rule over them, bring them here and slay them before me.

When he had said these things, he went on before them, going up to Jerusalem.

CHAPTER XIV

THE LAST PUBLIC MINISTRY IN JERUSALEM

Section 133. Jesus Arrives at Bethany

John 11:55 to 12:1

The Passover of the Jews was approaching. Many went up to Jerusalem from the country before the Passover that they might purify themselves. They kept seeking Jesus and saying to one another while standing in the temple, What do you think? That he will not come to the feast? For the chief priests and Pharisees had given orders that any one who knew where he was should tell it so that they might arrest him.

Six days before the Passover, Jesus came to Bethany, where Lazarus, whom Jesus had raised from the dead, lived.

Section 134. Mary Anoints Jesus at Simon's House

Mark 14:3-9. Matthew 26:6-13. John 12:2-11

There, they made a supper for him in the house of Simon the leper.[1] Martha was serving, but Lazarus was one of those who reclined at the table with him.

While he reclined, Mary, having an alabaster flask containing a pound of ointment of spikenard, genuine and very precious, took it, broke it, and poured it over his head and anointed the feet of Jesus and wiped his feet with her hair. The house was filled with the fragrance of the ointment.

Judas Iscariot, one of his disciples (he who was going to betray him) was filled with indignation and said, To what purpose

---

1. John and Mark (since Matthew only follows Mark) disagree in the time of this Supper. Mark places it just two days before the crucifixion and sets it forth as the immediate cause of the betrayal by Judas. Of course, it is impossible to settle with certainty the exact time, most scholars following Mark's order. However, I have felt that John's should be followed. First, John is careful to give the exact time of the Supper and is found in our study to be correct in such matters usually. Second, no explanation can be offered as to why John should set this back, while Mark is justified in setting it up to show one of the causes for the betrayal.

was this waste of perfume made? Why was it not sold for sixty dollars and given to the poor?

This he said, not because he cared for the poor, but because he was a thief. He carried the money bag and was in the habit of taking out what was put in it.

So they all began to murmur at her.

Jesus, knowing it, said to them, Why do you trouble the woman? Leave her alone. She has performed a good work on me. You will always have the poor with you, and when you want to, you can do something for them. But you do not always have me. She has done what she could: she poured this ointment on my body to prepare it for the day of burial. I tell you truly that wherever this gospel shall be proclaimed in the whole world, this thing that she has done will also be spoken of as a memorial for her.

A great crowd of Jews learned that he was there, and they came out, not only on account of Jesus, but also that they might see Lazarus whom he had raised from the dead. Then the chief priests took counsel as to how they might put Lazarus to death also, for many of the Jews were going away and believing in Jesus on his account.

Section 135. The Triumphal Entry

Mark 11:1-11. Matthew 21:1-11, 14-17.
Luke 19:29-44. John 12:12-19

On the morrow a great crowd which had come to the feast heard that Jesus was coming to Jerusalem and they took branches of palm trees and went out to meet him.

When he had come near to Bethpage and Bethany, to the Mount of Olives, he sent two of his disciples, saying to them, Go into the village ahead of you, and as soon as you enter it, you will find a donkey tied, and her colt with her on whom no man ever sat. Untie it and bring it to me. If anyone should say, Why do you do this? Say, The Lord has need of it. He will send them here at once.

The disciples went and did as Jesus had commanded them. They found the donkey tied to the door outside on the street, and they untied the colt.

Those standing there, the owners, said, Why are you untying the colt?

They said to them, The Lord has need of it.

Then they allowed them to go. They brought the donkey and the colt to Jesus and put their garments on it, and Jesus sat on it. This was done that the word spoken through the prophet might be fulfilled, saying:

> Speak to the daughter of Zion,
> Lo, your king comes to you,
> Meek and riding upon a donkey,
> Upon the colt, the foal of a donkey.

His disciples did not understand this at first, but when Jesus was glorified, they remembered that this was written of him and that they had done these things for him.

The crowd which was with him when he called Lazarus from the grave and raised him from the dead kept telling it. This was why the crowd met him, for they had heard that he had done this sign. The Pharisees therefore said to one another, See, you accomplish nothing. Lo, the world has gone after him.

As they went on, most of the crowd spread their own garments in the way; others cut branches from the trees in the fields and spread them in the way. When he drew near, even to the descent of the Mount of Olives, all the multitude of his disciples—those going before and those coming after—began to rejoice and praise God with a great voice for all the wonders which they had seen, saying:

> Hosanna to the Son of David!
> Blessed is he who comes in the name of the Lord,
> Even the King of Israel.
> Hosanna in the highest!
> Peace in heaven and glory in the highest!

Some of the Pharisees in the crowd said to him, Teacher, rebuke your disciples.

He answered, I tell you that if these were silent, the stones would cry out.

As he drew near, he saw the city and wept over it, saying, If you had known, even you, on this day what things make for peace! But now they have been hidden from your eyes. The days are coming upon you when your enemies will cast up a rampart about you and will encircle you and hem you in all around. They will dash you and your children with you to the ground, and they will not leave a stone upon a stone within you, for you did not know the time of your visitation.

When he came into Jerusalem, the whole city was astir, saying, Who is this?

The crowd kept saying, This is the prophet, Jesus of Nazareth of Galilee. The blind came to him, and the lame, in the temple. And he healed them. But the chief priests and scribes, seeing the wonderful things which he did and hearing the children cry out in the temple:

> Hosanna to the Son of David,

were indignant, and said to him, Do you hear what these are saying?

Jesus said to them, Yes! Have you never read:

> Out of the mouths of babes and sucklings,
> You have perfected praise?

When he had looked around at all things, it being late in the evening, he went out to Bethany and lodged there with the twelve.

Section 136. THE FIG TREE CURSED: THE TEMPLE CLEANSED

Mark 11:12-18.   Matthew 21:12-13, 18-19a.
Luke 19:45-48

The next day when they were coming from Bethany, he was hungry. Seeing a fig tree in leaf at some distance, he went to see if he might find something on it; but when he reached it, he found nothing but leaves, for it was not the season for figs. He said to it, May no one ever eat fruit from you again.

His disciples heard it.

He came into Jerusalem and entered the temple and began to cast out all who were buying and selling in the temple. He overturned the tables of those that changed money, the seats of them that sold doves, and would not allow anyone to carry a vessel through the temple. Then he began to teach them, saying, Is it not written: My house shall be called a house of prayer among all the nations? Yet, you have made it a den of robbers.

He was teaching daily in the temple, but the chief priests and leading men of the people kept seeking a way to destroy him. They were afraid of him, for all the people were amazed at his doctrine. But they could find no way to do it because all the people were hanging on his words.

Section 137. THE GREEKS SEEK HIM

John 12:20-50

There were some Greeks among those who had come up to worship at the feast.[2] These came to Philip who was from Bethsaida of Galilee, and said to him, Sir, we would like to see Jesus.

---

2. The incident of the Greek's seeking to see Jesus was placed on his second day in Jerusalem because it is thought that they would do this as soon as possible. It could not be placed more than two days later. The decision is not vital in any case. It is recorded only by John, and no contact with the Synoptic accounts gives a clue to its proper order.

Philip went and told Andrew; Andrew and Philip came and told Jesus.

Jesus answered them, The hour has come for the Son of man to be glorified. Truly, truly, I tell you, if a grain of wheat does not fall into the ground and die, it abides alone. But if it dies, it bears much fruit. He who loves his life loses it, but he who hates his life in this world will keep it unto eternal life. If anyone would serve me, let him follow me, and where I am, there also my servant will be. If anyone serves me, the Father will honor him. My soul is troubled; what shall I say? Father, save me from this hour? No, it was for this that I came to this hour. Father, glorify thy name.

Then there came a voice out of heaven, I have both glorified it and will glorify it again.

The crowd which stood around and heard it said, It thundered.

But others said, An angel has spoken to him.

Jesus replied, It was not for my sake but for yours that this voice came. Now is this world judged; now the prince of this world will be cast out; and I, if I be lifted up from the earth, will draw all men to myself.

This he said to show what kind of death he was going to die.

The crowd therefore answered, We have learned from our law that the Messiah will abide forever. How do you say that it is necessary for the Son of man to be lifted up? Who is this Son of man?

Jesus said to them, Still a little while is the light with you. Walk according to the light that you have so that the darkness will not overcome you; he who walks in the darkness does not know where he is going. While you have the light, believe in the light, so that you may become sons of light.

After Jesus had said this, he went away and hid from them.

Even though he had done such signs before them, they did not believe on him, that the word of Isaiah the prophet might be fulfilled which he spoke:

Lord, who has believed our report?
To whom has the arm of the Lord been revealed?

Therefore, they could not believe for Isaiah said again:

He has blinded their eyes and hardened their hearts,
Lest seeing with their eyes, and
Understanding with their hearts,
And turning, I should heal them.

Isaiah spoke these things about him, for he had seen his glory. Nevertheless, even of the rulers many believed in him, but because of the Pharisees they did not confess him lest they should be excommunicated. For they loved the praise of men more than the praise of God.

Jesus cried out, He who believes in me believes not in me but in him who sent me, and he who sees me sees him who sent me. I have come as light to the world so that everyone who believes in me will not abide in darkness. If a man hears my words and does not keep them, I will not judge him; I came not to judge the world but to save the world. He who rejects me and receives not my words has one who judges him. The word which I have spoken will judge him in the last day. I have not spoken on my own authority, but the Father who sent me has told me what to say and what to speak. I know that his commandment is eternal life. Therefore what I speak, I speak just as the Father has told me.

Section 138. The Fig Tree Is Found Withered

Mark 11:19-25.   Matthew 21:19b-22.   Luke 21:37-38

His habit was to teach by day in the temple and go out every evening from the city and lodge during the night on the Mount of Olives. So all the people made it a habit to come early to the temple to hear him.

Early the next morning, when they passed by, they saw that the fig tree had withered away at once from the root. When they saw it, the disciples marveled, saying, How did the fig tree wither so soon? Peter reminded him and said, Rabbi, lo, the fig tree which you cursed is withered away.

Jesus answered, Have faith in God. I tell you truly that if you have faith and doubt not, you cannot only do what was done to the fig tree, but you can even say to this mountain, Be lifted up and be cast into the sea. If you doubt not, but believe that what you have said will happen, it will. I say to you, anything that you ask when you are praying, believe that you have received it, and it will be yours. When you stand praying, forgive if you have any grievance against anyone, so that your Father in heaven may forgive you your trespasses.

Section 139. A CHALLENGE OF THE AUTHORITY OF JESUS

Mark 11:27-33.   Matthew 21:23-32.   Luke 20:1-8

They came to Jerusalem. While he was walking in the temple, teaching and preaching the gospel, the chief priests and the scribes and elders came to him and said, Tell us, what authority do you have to do these things? Who gave you this authority that you may do them?

Jesus answered them, I will ask you one question: you answer me, and I will tell you by what authority I do these things. The baptism of John, where did it come from? From heaven or from men? Answer me.

They began to debate among themselves, If we say, From heaven, he will say, Why then did you not believe him? But, if we say, from men, the people will all stone us. They feared the people for they all held that John was truly a prophet.

So they answered Jesus, We do not know.

Jesus said to them, Neither will I tell you by what authority I do these things. What do you think? A man had two sons

He came to the first and said, Son, go and work in the vineyard today. He answered, I will, sir, but he did not go. Then he came to the second and said the same thing. He answered, I will not, but later he repented and went. Which of the two sons did the will of the father?

They said, The last.

Jesus said to them, Truly I tell you that the tax-collectors and harlots will go into the kingdom of God before you. John came to you in the way of righteousness and you did not believe him. The tax-collectors and harlots did believe him. But even when you saw this, you did not afterward repent and believe in him.

Section 140. The Parable of the Vineyard

Mark 12:1-12.   Matthew 21:33-46.   Luke 20:9-19

Listen to another parable. Then he began to speak to the people this parable: There was a man who was a householder. He planted a vineyard, set a hedge around it, digged a pit for a winepress, and built a tower. Then he rented it out to tenants and went into another country for a long time.

When the time of fruit drew near, he sent slaves to the tenants to receive from them the rent portion of the fruit of the vineyard. But the tenants took his slaves; one they beat; one they killed; the other they stoned.

Again he sent other slaves, more than at first. These they also beat on the head and handled shamefully and sent away empty.

He sent others of whom they beat some and killed some.

The master of the vineyard said, What can I do? I will send my son whom I love. Surely they will respect him.

He sent him last of all. But those tenants reasoned among themselves, This is the heir. Come! Let us kill him and we will be the heirs. So they cast him outside the vineyard and killed him. What will the master of the vineyard do? He will come and destroy those tenants and rent the vineyard to other tenants who will render fruit to him in its season.

When they heard it, they said, God forbid.

But looking on them, Jesus said, Why then is it written:

> The stone which the builders rejected,
> The same is made the head of the corner.
> This was from the Lord,
> It is marvelous in our eyes?

Therefore, I tell you that the kingdom of God will be taken from you and given to a nation producing its fruits. He who falls upon this stone will be broken to pieces, but whoever it falls upon will be crushed to powder.

When the chief priests and Pharisees heard his parables, they knew that he spoke concerning them. But when they tried to arrest him, they were afraid of the people, for they held him to be a prophet. So they left and went away.

Section 141. THE PARABLE OF THE KING'S FEAST

Matthew 22:14

Jesus again spoke to them a parable: The kingdom of heaven is like a king who gave a marriage feast for his son. He sent his slaves to call those who were invited to the marriage feast, but they refused to come. Again he sent out slaves, saying, Tell those who are invited, Behold I have made my dinner ready, my oxen and my fatlings are killed, and all things are ready. Come to the feast.

They, not caring, went their way: one to his own field, another to his merchandise. The rest laid hold on his slaves and insulted them and killed them.

This enraged the king, and he sent his soldiers and destroyed those murderers and burned their city.

Then he said to his slaves, The feast is ready and those who were invited were not worthy. Go into the crossroads and invite anyone you find to the wedding feast.

Those slaves went into the way and brought all they found, both good and bad, so the wedding hall was filled with guests.

When the king came to see those who reclined at the tables, he saw there a man who was not dressed in a wedding garment. He said to him, Friend, how is it that you came here without a wedding garment?

He was speechless.

Then the king said to the attendants, Bind him hand and foot; cast him out into the outer darkness where there will be weeping and gnashing of teeth.

So many are called but few are chosen.

Section 142. About Paying Taxes

Mark 12:13-17. Matthew 22:15-22. Luke 20:20-26

The Pharisees took counsel how to ensnare him in his speech. They watched him and sent spies to pretend to be sincere so they could trap him in a word and hand him over to the rule and authority of the governor. Some were their disciples, and some were Herodians. When they came, they said, Teacher, we know that you tell and teach the truth without regard to any man's position, but teach the way of God in truth. Tell us therefore what you think. Is it lawful to pay taxes to Caesar or not? Should we pay it, or should we refuse?

Jesus knew their evil intention and said, Why do you tempt me, you hypocrites? Bring me a coin that I may see it.

They brought him one.   He said, Whose picture and inscription does it bear?

They said, Caesar's.

He said, Pay Caesar the things which belong to Caesar; but pay God what belongs to God.

They could not dispute his saying before the people.   So, marveling at him, they went away in silence.

Section 143. ABOUT THE RESURRECTION

Mark 12:18-27.   Matthew 22:23-33.   Luke 20:27-40

On that same day some of the Sadducees, who say there is no resurrection, came up and asked him, Teacher, Moses wrote, If one's brother should die and leave a widow but not a child, his brother should take the widow and raise up seed to his brother.   There were with us seven brothers.   The first took a wife and died childless.   Then the second took her and died childless also.   Likewise the third.   All the seven died without leaving a child.   Finally the woman died.   In the resurrection, therefore, to which of the seven will she be married?   For all of the seven married her.

Jesus said to them, You go astray because you do not know the Scriptures nor the power of God.   The sons of this world marry and give in marriage, but those who attain the coming world by the resurrection of the dead neither marry nor give in marriage.   Neither will they die any more, for they are equal to the angels, and are sons of God, being sons of the resurrection.

But concerning the dead, that they will rise again, have you not read in the book of Moses how God said to him at the burning bush, I am the God of Abraham, the God of Isaac, and the God of Jacob?   Now he is not the God of dead but of living men, for all live in him.   You do greatly err.

When the crowd heard it, they were greatly astonished at his teaching.   Some of the scribes answered, Teacher, you speak the truth.   They no longer dared to ask him anything.

Section 144. ABOUT THE GREAT COMMANDMENT

Mark 12:28-34.   Matthew 22:34-40

The Pharisees, hearing that he had put the Sadducees to silence, came together to him.   One of them who was a lawyer, tempting him, asked, Teacher, which commandment of the law is most important?

Jesus answered, The most important is:

Hear, O Israel, The Lord our God is one Lord,
And you shall love your Lord God with all your heart,
All your soul, all your mind,
And all your strength.

This is the first and most important commandment.   Another one like it comes second:

You shall love your neighbor as yourself.

There is no other commandment greater than these, for on these two commandments hang the whole law and the prophets.

One of the scribes, seeing that he had answered well, said, Well said, Teacher, of a truth you say that he is one and besides him there is no other.   And to love him with all the heart and all the understanding and all the strength and to love one's neighbor as one's self is much more than all the whole burnt offerings and sacrifices.

Jesus, seeing that he answered wisely, said to him, You are not far from the kingdom of God.

No one dared any longer to ask him anything.

Section 145. JESUS ASKS A QUESTION ABOUT DAVID'S SON

Mark 12:35-37.   Matthew 22:41-46.   Luke 20:41-44

While the Pharisees were still gathered together, Jesus asked them, What do you think about the Messiah?   Whose son is he?

They said, The son of David.

He said, How then could David speak by the Spirit and call him Lord, saying:

> The Lord said to my Lord,
> Sit at my right hand,
> Till I put your enemies under your feet?

Since David therefore called him Lord, how can he be his son?

No one was able to answer him a word, neither did anyone from that day on dare to ask him anything.

But the common people heard him gladly.

Section 146. THE SCRIBES AND PHARISEES DENOUNCED

Mark 12:38-40. Matthew 23:1-39. Luke 20:45-47

While all the people were listening, he said to his disciples, Beware of the scribes and Pharisees. They sit in the seat of Moses. Therefore practice and keep everything they tell you, but do not practice their works. For they say and do not. They bind heavy burdens and place them upon the shoulders of men, but they themselves are not willing to move them with their finger. They do all of their works to be seen of men. They make broad their phylacteries and the borders of their garments they make great and like to walk around in long robes. They love the chief place at the feasts and the chief seats in the synagogues and the greetings in the market places and to be called by men, Rabbi.

You shall not be called Rabbi. For one is your teacher and all of you are brothers.

Call no man on earth, Father. For one is your heavenly Father.

Neither be you called leader. For one is your leader, even the Messiah.

He that is greatest among you shall be your servant. For whoever exalts himself will be humbled, and whoever humbles himself will be exalted.

Woe to you, scribes and Pharisees, hypocrites! You shut the kingdom of heaven against men. You will neither enter it nor let those who wish to come in enter. You devour widows' houses even while making long prayers for a pretence. These (prayers) will receive the greater condemnation.

Woe to you, scribes and Pharisees, hypocrites! You travel over sea and land to make one proselyte, and when you have gained him, you make him twice as much a son of hell as yourselves.

Woe to you, blind guides! You say, Whoever swears by the temple; it is nothing. But whoever swears by the gold of the temple is bound by his oath. You blind fools, which is greater, the gold or the temple which makes the gold sacred? You say, Whoever swears by the altar; it is nothing. But whoever swears by the gift that is on it is bound by his oath. You blind men, which is greater, the gift or the altar which makes the gift sacred? Therefore, he who swears by the altar, swears both by it and by all that is on it. And he who swears by the temple swears by it and all that is housed in it. And he that swears by heaven swears by the throne of God and by him who sits upon it.

Woe to you, scribes and Pharisees, hypocrites! You give tithes of mint and dill and cummin, and have left off the more vital matters of the law—justice and mercy and faithfulness. These things ye ought to do and not leave off the others. You blind guides, you strain out a gnat and drink a camel down.

Woe to you, scribes and Pharisees, hypocrites! You cleanse the outside of the cup and the platter, but within they are full of extortion and excess. You blind Pharisees! first cleanse the inside of the cup that the outside may also become clean.

Woe to you, scribes and Pharisees, hypocrites! You are like whitewashed tombs, which indeed appear beautiful on the outside, but on the inside they are full of dead men's bones and all uncleanness. Likewise, you appear outwardly to be righteous to men, but within you are full of hypocrisy and wickedness.

Woe to you, scribes and Pharisees, hypocrites! You build the tombs of the prophets and decorate the graves of the righteous, and say, If we had lived in the days of our fathers we would not have shared with them in the blood of the prophets. Thus you testify against yourselves, for you are sons of the murderers of the prophets. You fill up the measure of your fathers. You serpents, you children of vipers, how can you escape the judgment of hell? Lo, I send you prophets and wise men and scribes; some of them you will kill and crucify; some of them you will scourge in your synagogues and persecute from city to city. Thus will come upon you all the righteous blood shed upon the earth from the blood of righteous Abel to the blood of Zachariah the son Barachiah, whom you murdered between the temple and the altar.

Truly I tell you, all these things will come upon this generation.

Jerusalem, Jerusalem, you who killed the prophets and stoned those who were sent to you, how often have I wished to gather your sons together as a hen gathers her young under her wings, but you would not. Lo, I leave you your house. For I say to you, You will never see me until the time when you say:

Blessed is he who comes in the name of the Lord.

Section 147. JESUS COMMENDS THE POOR WIDOW'S GIFT

Mark 12:41-44. Luke 21:1-4

He sat down by the treasury and watched the people put money into the treasury. Looking up, he saw many who were rich putting in large gifts. He saw a poor widow come and put in two small coins which hardly make a penny.

He called his disciples and said to them, I tell you of a truth that this poor widow has put in more than all the others who put money into the treasury. They all out of their abundance put in their gifts, but she out of her want has put in all that she had, all of her living.

CHAPTER XV

IN THE SHADOW WITH JESUS

Section 148. PROPHECIES OF THE FUTURE

Mark 13:1-37. Matthew 24:1-41; 10:16-23. Luke 21:5-36

/ As Jesus went out of the temple, his disciples were showing him the building of the temple that it was adorned with beautiful stones and offerings, and one of them said, Teacher, see what manner of stones and what manner of building.

Jesus said to him, You see these great buildings, do you not? I tell you truly, the days will come when one stone will not be left upon another stone which will not be thrown down.

While he was sitting on the Mount of Olives facing the temple, Peter, James, John, and Andrew asked him privately about these things, saying, Teacher, tell us when these things will be and what the sign of your coming and the consumation of the age is.

Jesus began to say to them, Take heed that no man lead you astray. Many will come in my name, saying, I am the Messiah and the time is near, and many will be led astray. But do not follow them. When you hear of wars and tumults and rumors of wars, stop being alarmed. These things must come first, but the end does not follow immediately.

He continued, Nation will rise up against nation and kingdom against kingdom, and great earthquakes will come, and there will be famines and pestilence in many places, also terrors and great signs from heaven. These are the beginning of sufferings.

Behold, I send you out as sheep among wolves; become as wise as serpents and as harmless as doves. Beware of men, for they will arrest you and persecute you. They will deliver you up to the councils; and in their synagogues, they will scourge you. They will cast you in prison and kill you. Yes, you will

[167]

stand before governors and kings as witness to them and to the nations. And all the world will hate you for my sake. Many false prophets will arise and lead many astray. Because wickedness will be multiplied, the love of many will grow cold. But he that endures to the end, the same will be saved. This gospel of the kingdom will be preached in the whole world for a testimony unto all nations; then the end will come.

When they lead you away to deliver you, be not troubled beforehand about how or what you will speak. For speech and wisdom will be given you in that hour which adversaries will not be able to deny nor withstand. You will not be the one who speaks, but the Spirit of your Father will speak through you. Many will stumble and hate one another and deliver up one another. Brother will deliver up brother to death, and a father his child. Children will also rise up against parents and put them to death. You will be hated by all men for my name's sake. But not a hair of your head will be destroyed. In your endurance you will preserve your lives.

When they persecute you in this city, flee to another. I tell you of a truth, you will not have gone through the cities of Israel before the Son of man comes.

When therefore you see the abomination of desolation—spoken of through Daniel the prophet—standing in the holy place where he ought not (Let him that reads understand) and when you see Jerusalem surrounded with armies, know that the time of her desolation is near. Let them that are in Judea flee to the mountains, and those who are in the midst of her go out. Let not those who are in the country come in. He that is on the housetop, let him not come down to take up the things in his house, and he who is in the field, let him not return again to take his coat. These are days of vengeance, that all things which are written may be fulfilled.

Woe to those who are with child and those who give suck in those days! Pray that your flight will not be in the winter or on the sabbath. For then great tribulation would be. In those days will be great tribulation such as has not happened from the beginning of the world which God created until now, and will never be. Except those days had been shortened, no flesh at all would survive. But for the sake of the elect, those days will be shortened.

There will be great distress upon the land and wrath on this people. They will fall by the edge of the sword, and will be led captive into all the nations; Jerusalem will be trodden down by the Gentiles until the time of the Gentiles is fulfilled.

If any man shall say to you, Lo, here is the Messiah; lo, there; believe him not. False Messiahs and false prophets will arise and give great signs and wonders so as to lead astray even the elect if it were possible. Beware, I have told you all things beforehand. If therefore they shall say to you, Lo, he is in the wilderness, go not out; lo, in the private room, believe him not; for as the lightening comes from the east and shines to the west, so will it be at the coming of the Son of man. Wherever the carcase is, there will the vultures gather together.

Immediately after those days of tribulation, the sun will be darkened; the moon will fail to give her light; the stars will fall from the heavens; there will be distress of nations upon the earth from perplexity caused by the roaring of the sea and the billows; and men will faint from fear of the things that come upon the world. The very powers of heaven will be shaken. Then the sign of the Son of man will appear in heaven, and all the tribes of the earth will mourn because they see the Son of man coming with the clouds of heaven with great power and glory. He will send his angels with a mighty sound of the trumpet, and they will gather together his elect from the four winds, from the ends of the earth to the ends of heaven.

When these things begin to happen, look up and lift up your heads, for your redemption is drawing near.

Learn a parable from the fig tree and all the trees. When their branches become tender and begin to put on leaves, you know of yourselves that summer is near. Likewise when you see all things coming to pass, know that the kingdom of God is near, even at the door. I tell you truly that this generation will not pass away before all these things are accomplished. Heaven and earth will pass away, but my words will never pass away.

Concerning that day and hour, no man knows; no, not the angels of heaven nor the Son, only the Father. As the days of Noah were, so will the coming of the Son of man be. Just as in the days before the flood, they were eating and drinking, marrying and giving in marriage, until the day when Noah entered the ark, and knew not of it until the flood came and took them all away, so will the coming of the Son of man be Two men will be in the field; one will be taken and one left. Two women will be grinding at the mill; one will be taken and one left.

Watch therefore, lest, your hearts being loaded by debauchery and drunkenness and anxieties of life, that day should come upon you as a trap. For it will come upon all those who dwell upon the face of the earth.

Take heed! Watch! for you know not when the time is. It will be like it is when a man leaves his house and gives his slaves authority, to each one his work, and commands the porter to watch, then takes a journey to another country. Watch therefore, for you know not when the master of the house comes, whether at evening or midnight or cock-crowing or early morning; lest coming suddenly, he should find you sleeping. Watch at every season, making supplication, that you may be able to escape all these things which are going to happen and stand before the Son of man.

What I tell you, I tell all, Watch!

Section 149. THREE PARABLES OF THE END

Matthew 25:1-46

The Ten Virgins

The kingdom of heaven will be like ten virgins, who took their lamps and went out to meet the bridegroom. Five of them were foolish and five were wise. The foolish took their lamps but took no oil with them. The wise took cans of oil with their lamps. While the bridegroom delayed they all nodded and were sleeping. At midnight a cry came, Lo, the bridegroom, Come to meet him.

All those virgins arose and trimmed their lamps. The foolish said to the wise, Give us some of your oil, for our lamps have gone out.

The wise answered, No, lest there be not enough for us and you. Go rather to those who sell and buy from them.

While they were gone to buy, the bridegroom came, and those who were ready entered with him into the wedding feast and the door was shut.

Afterward the rest of the virgins came, saying, Lord, Lord, open to us!

He answered, I tell you truly that I do not know you.

Watch therefore! for you know not the day nor the hour.

The Talents

It is just like a man traveling into a far country, who called his own slaves and committed to them his goods. To one he gave five thousand dollars. To one he gave two thousand. To the other he gave one thousand. To each one he gave according to his ability, then he departed.

Immediately the one who had received five thousand went and engaged in business with it and gained five more.

Likewise the one who received two gained two more.

But the one who had received one went and digged in the earth and hid his master's money.

After a long time, the master of those slaves came and made a reckoning with them.

The one who had received five thousand dollars came and brought five thousand more to him, saying, Master you gave me five thousand dollars. Lo, I have gained five thousand more.

His master said to him, Well done, good and faithful slave, over a little you have been faithful; I will give you authority over much. Enter into the joy of your master.

He who received two thousand dollars came and said, Master, you gave me two thousand dollars. Lo, I have gained two thousand more.

His master said to him, Well done, good and faithful slave, over a little you have been faithful; I will give you authority over much. Enter into the joy of your master.

Then the one who had received one thousand came and said, Master, I know that you are a stern man, reaping where you did not sow and gathering where you did not scatter. So, being afraid, I went and hid your thousand dollars in the ground. Lo, you have what is yours.

His master answered him, You wicked and slothful slave. Did you know that I reaped what I had not sown and that I gather where I have not scattered? You ought therefore to have put my money in the bank, and then when I came, I could have received my own with interest. Therefore, take the thousand dollars away from him and give it to him who has ten thousand. To him that has, all things will be given and he will have an abundance. But from him who has not, even what he has will be taken from him. Cast the unprofitable slave into the outer darkness. There will be weeping and gnashing of teeth there.

The Final Judgment

When the Son of man comes in his glory and all the angels with him, then will he sit upon his throne of glory. All the nations will be gathered before him, and he will divide them from one another, as the shepherd separates the sheep from the goats; the sheep will stand on his right hand, but the goats on his left hand.

The king will then say to those on his right hand, Come, you blessed of my Father, inherit the kingdom prepared for you from the foundation of the world. When I was hungry, you gave me food. I was thirsty, and you gave me drink; I was a stranger, and you took me in; I was naked, and you clothed me; I was sick, and you visited me; I was in prison, and you came to me.

Then will the righteous answer him, Lord, when did we see you hungry and fed you? or thirsty and gave you drink? When did we see you a stranger and took you in? or naked and clothed you? When did we see you sick or in prison and came to you?

The king will answer them, I tell you truly, inasmuch as you did it to one of the least of these my brothers, you did it unto me.

Then will he say to those on his left hand, Depart from me you cursed, into everlasting fire which has been prepared for the devil and his angels. I was hungry, and you gave me no food; I was thirsty, and you gave me nothing to drink; I was a stranger, and you took me not in; I was naked, and you did not clothe me; I was sick and in prison, and you did not visit me.

Then will these also answer, Lord, when did we see you hungry or thirsty or a stranger or naked or sick or in prison, and did not minister to you?

He will answer them, I tell you truly, inasmuch as you did not do it to one of the least of these, you did not do it to me.

These will go away into eternal punishment, but the righteous to eternal life.

Section 150. Jesus Predicts the Time of His Death
Mark 14:1-2. Matthew 25:1-5. Luke 22:1-2

When Jesus had finished all these words, he said to his disciples, You know that after two days the Passover and the feast of the unleavened bread comes, and the Son of man will be delivered up to be crucified.

The chief priests and the scribes and the elders of the people were gathered together to the palace of the high priest, whose name was Caiaphas, and they took counsel together how they might arrest Jesus by guile and put him to death. But they said, Not during the feast lest a tumult arise among the people.

For they feared the people.

Section 151. JUDAS BARGAINS TO BETRAY JESUS

Mark 14:10-11.   Matthew 26:14-16.   Luke 22:3-6

Satan entered into Judas Iscariot, one of the twelve, and he went and conspired with the chief priests and captains to deliver him to them.   He said, What will you give me to deliver him?

When they heard it, they rejoiced and were glad to give him money.   So they weighed out thirty pieces of silver to him.

He sought an opportunity to deliver him to them in the absence of the crowd.

Section 152. THE NEW TENDERNESS OF JESUS

John 13:1

Before the feast of the Passover, Jesus knowing that his hour had come to depart from this world to the Father, and having loved his own while in the world, he loved them to the end.[1]

Section 153. PREPARATION FOR THE PASSOVER MEAL

Mark 14:12-16.   Matthew 26:17-19.   Luke 22:7-13

On the first day of the unleavened bread[2] when the Passover must be sacrificed, the disciples of Jesus said to him, Where do you want us to make preparation to eat the Passover.

---

1. This is a summary statement of the new tenderness of Jesus toward his disciples as he faced the coming crisis of his life.   It is an independent statement and does not properly belong, in point of time, with what follows in John.

2. There is a point of debate as to the accuracy of John in recording the Passover.   All the Gospels give it on the evening before the crucifixion, and the Synoptics make it plain that this is the regular time for the Passover.   Some have insisted that John makes it come a day earlier than the regular Jewish Passover.   One of the passages taken to prove this discrepancy is John 13:1, which the above note points out is a summary statement.   Another is the admonition of Jesus to Judas in John 13:27.   "That thou doest, do quickly."   But this could hardly mean that Judas is to hurry out and buy materials for a meal which was to come twenty-four hours later.   The disciples thought Jesus told him to go out and buy supplies for the feast; this undoubtedly means the Feast of Unleavened Bread.   Another point is the refusal of the Pharisees to enter into the palace of the governor because it would disqualify them from eating the Passover (John 18:28).   Here again the Feast of Unleavened Bread, following the Passover, is meant.   If it were the morning of the Passover, any defilement would pass away at six o'clock in the evening.   Hence their scruples would have been without point.   Another passage often quoted is John 19:14, "It was the Preparation of the Passover."   Some who are unfamiliar with Jewish custom suppose this to mean the day when the Passover was being prepared for.   However, this is a technical term for our Friday, the preparation for the sabbath, and the expression means that it was Friday of Passover week.   John 19:31 says, "The day of that sabbath was a high day."   From this, some have supposed that the Passover and the sabbath coincided that year.   This is gratuitous reasoning, however, since the sabbath of the feast week would be a high day.   In the light of the evidence, there are no grounds for supposing John and the Synoptics to be in contradiction.

He sent Peter and John, saying to them, Go and prepare the Passover for us to eat.   When you enter into the city, a man will meet you, carrying a pitcher of water.   Follow him to the house into which he will enter and say to the master of the house, The Teacher says, My time is near.   I wish to keep the Passover at your house.   Where is my guest chamber where I may eat the Passover with my disciples.   He will himself show you a large upper room prepared; there prepare for us.

So the disciples went out and came into the city and found it just as Jesus had told them, and they prepared the Passover.

Section 154. Jesus Rebukes the Twelve for Jealousy

Mark 14:17.   Matthew 26:20.   Luke 22:14-16, 24-30

When the evening came, he came with the twelve disciples.[3] When the hour had come, he reclined at the table and his apostles with him.   He said to them, I have earnestly desired to eat this Passover meal with you before I suffer, for I tell you that I will never eat it again until it is fulfilled in the kingdom of God.

There arose a strife among them as to which would rank the highest.   He said to them, The kings of the Gentiles lord it over them, and those who have authority over them are called benefactors.   But you are not so.   Rather, he who is greatest among you, let him continue to be as the youngest; and he who governs let him be as a servant.   For which is greater, the one who reclines at the table or the one who serves?   Is not he who reclines?   I am in the midst of you as one who serves.   You

3. In the Passion Week material, we come nearer to having four independent accounts than in any other place.   It is to be expected that when this is true, minor details will differ. The judgment of the student must be used in arranging these details.   A point which illustrates this is the four records of the last night of Jesus' ministry, beginning with the preparation for eating the Passover.   For instance, each writer records the denial of Peter three times. The details, however, do not fit into place.   When we remember the rapidity of movement, the emotional stress of these hours, and the bewilderment of the disciples, this is only natural. The trial of Jesus passed through three stages involving several hours of time.   The denials of Peter were probably parallel to these stages of time.   But agreement is present in the broad outlines of the account and the arrangement in the text of this work seems correct to me.

are the ones who have continued with me through my trials.
I will bestow royal power on you just as my Father bestowed it
on me that you may eat and drink at my table in my kingdom.
You will sit upon thrones judging the twelve tribes of Israel.

Section 155. Jesus Washes the Disciples' Feet

John 13:2-20

When the supper arrived—the devil having already put it
into the heart of Judas Iscariot, the son of Simon, to betray
him—Jesus, knowing that the Father had given all things into
his hands and that he had come from God and was going to
God, arose from the table, laid aside his garments, and girded
himself with a towel. Then he put water into a basin and
began to wash the feet of the disciples and dry them with the
towel with which he was girded. He came therefore to Simon
Peter.

He said to him, Lord, do you wash my feet?

Jesus answered, What I do, you do not understand. But
you will know later.

Peter said to him, You will never wash my feet.

Jesus answered, If I do not wash you, you have no part with
me.

Simon Peter said to him, Lord, not my feet only but my
hands and my head.

Jesus said to him, He that is bathed has no need except that
his feet be washed, but is wholly clean. You are clean, but not
all of you.

He knew him who should betray him. Therefore he said,
You are not all clean.

When he had washed their feet, he took his garments and
reclined at the table again. He said to them, Do you know

what I have done to you? You call me, Teacher and Lord, and you speak right, for I am. If therefore I, the Lord and Teacher, have washed your feet, you ought to wash one another's feet. For I have given you an example that you should do as I have done to you.

Truly, truly, I tell you, the slave is not greater than his master, nor the apostle greater than he who sent him. If you know these things, happy are you if you practice them. I do not speak concerning all of you; I know whom I have chosen; that the Scripture might be fulfilled:

> He that eats my bread
> Has lifted up his heel against me.

From now on I tell you before it comes to pass so that when it does come to pass, you may believe that I am he. Truly, truly, I tell you, he that receives whomever I send receives me, and he that receives me receives him that sent me.

Section 156. JESUS POINTS OUT THE BETRAYER

Mark 14:18-21.   Matthew 26:21-25.
Luke 22:21-23.   John 13:21-30

While they were eating, Jesus was troubled in spirit and testified, Truly, truly, I tell you that one of you will betray me. Yes, lo, the hand of the betrayer is with mine on the table.

They began to question among themselves which of them it was who would do this thing. They looked on one another, doubting of whom he spoke. Being very sorrowful, they began each one to say to him, It is not I, Lord, is it?

There was reclining on his bosom one of the disciples whom Jesus loved. Simon Peter therefore beckoned to him and said, Ask him of whom he speaks.

He therefore, leaning back upon the breast of Jesus, said to him, Lord, who is it?

Jesus answered, It is one of the twelve.   He it is for whom I shall dip this morsel and give it to him.   Truly, the Son of man goes just as it is written concerning him.   But woe to the man through whom the Son of man is betrayed!   It would have been better for him if that man had not been born.

Dipping the morsel, he took it and gave it to Judas the son of Simon Iscariot.

Then Judas (he who betrayed him) said, It is not I, Rabbi, is it?

He said to him, You have said.

Then Satan entered into that one.   Jesus therefore said to him, What you do, do quickly!

But none of them who reclined at the table knew why he spoke thus to him.   Some thought, since Judas had the money bag, that Jesus said to him, Buy what we have need of for the feast; or, that he should give something to the poor.

Therefore, taking the morsel, he went out at once.   And it was night.

Section 157. Jesus Warns the Disciples Against Desertion

Mark 14:27-31.   Matthew 26:31-35.
Luke 22:31-38.   John 13:31-38

When he had gone out, Jesus said, Now is the Son of man glorified, and God is glorified in him.   God will glorify him in himself, and straightway will he glorify him.   Little children, yet a little while I am with you.   You will seek me, and just as I said to the Jews, Where I am you cannot come; now I tell you.   A new commandment I give to you that you love one another.   Just as I have loved you, you also love one another. In this all men will know that you are my disciples, if you have love one for another.

Simon Peter said to him, Lord, where are you going?

Jesus answered, Where I go you are not able to follow me now, but you will follow me later.

Peter said, Lord, why can I not follow you now?

Jesus said to them all, All of you will be offended in me this night, for it is written:

I will smite the shepherd,
And the sheep of the flock will be scattered abroad.

But after I am risen, I will go before you into Galilee.

Peter said, Though all men be offended in you, I will never be offended.

He said, Simon, Simon, lo, Satan has asked for you that he might sift you as wheat, but I made supplication for you that your faith might not fail. And you, when you turn back, strengthen your brothers.

He said, Lord, I am ready to go with you both to prison and to death. I will lay down my life for you.

Jesus said to him, Will you lay down your life for me? Truly, I tell you, Peter, this very night before the cock shall crow twice you will deny me three times.

Peter replied heatedly, If I must die with you, yet will I not deny you.

All the disciples said the same thing.

He said to them, When I sent you without purse and wallet and sandals, did you lack anything?

They said, Nothing.

He said to them, Now he who has a purse, take it; likewise also a wallet. He who has none, let him sell his cloke and buy

a sword.   I tell you that that which is written must be fulfilled
in me:

And he was counted with transgressors.

For what concerns me has fulfilment.

They said to him, Lord, see, here are two swords.

He said, It is enough.

Section 158. The Lord's Supper Is Instituted

Mark 14:22-25.   Matthew 26:26-29.   Luke 22:17-20

While they were eating, Jesus took bread and, having blessed
it, broke it, gave it to his disciples, and said, Take! Eat! This
is my body.

Taking the cup also and blessing it, he gave it to them,
saying, Drink of it, all of you.   This is the blood of my new
covenant which is shed for many for the remission of sins

Truly, I tell you that I will not drink from now on of the
fruit of the vine until the day when I drink it new with you
in the kingdom of my Father.

Section 159. Jesus' Farewell Address in the Upper Room

John 14:1-31

Stop letting your hearts be troubled; continue to believe in
God, believe also in me.   In my Father's house are many man-
sions.   If it were not so, I would have told you.   I go to prepare
a place for you; and if I go and prepare a place for you, I will
come again and receive you unto myself, that where I am,
there you may be also.   Where I go you know, and the way.

Thomas said to him, Lord, we do not even know where you
are going.   How can we know the way?

Jesus said to him, I am the way and the truth and the life. No man comes to the Father but by me. If you had known me, you would also have known my Father. From now on you know and have seen him.

Philip said to him, Lord, show us the Father and it will satisfy us.

Jesus said to him, Have I been so long a time with you, Philip, and yet have you not known me? He who has seen me has seen the Father. How then do you say, Show us the Father? Do you not believe that I am in the Father and the Father is in me? The words which I speak to you, I speak not of myself. The Father who abides in me does his works. Believe me that I am in the Father and the Father in me, or else, believe on account of the works. Truly, truly, I tell you, he that believes in me will do the works which I do, and greater than these will he do because I go to the Father. Whatever you ask in my name, this will I do that the Father may be glorified in the Son. If you ask anything in my name, I will do it.

If you love me, you will keep my commandments. I will ask the Father, and he will give you another Helper that he may be with you forever, the Spirit of Truth, whom the world cannot receive, for it neither sees nor knows him. But you know him; he abides with you and is in you. I will not leave you orphaned, I come to you. Still a little while and the world sees me no longer, but you will see me. Because I continue to live, you will live also. In that hour you will know that I am in my Father and you in me and I in you. He that has my commandments and keeps them, he is the one who loves me. He who loves me will be loved by my Father, and I will love him and will appear to him.

Judas (not Iscariot) said to him, Lord, How is it that you are going to reveal yourself to us and not to the world?

Jesus answered him, If any one loves me, he will keep my word, and my Father will love him, and we will come to him and we will make our home with him. He who does not love me does not keep my word. The word which you hear is not mine but my Father's who sent me. These things have I spoken to you while I am still with you. But the Helper, the Holy Spirit, whom the Father will send in my name, he will teach you all things and remind you of all things which I have said to you.

Peace I leave with you; my peace I give to you. Nor do I give to you as the world gives. Let not your hearts be troubled, neither let them be afraid. You have heard that I said, I go away and I come for you. If you loved me, you would have rejoiced that I go to the Father, for the Father is greater than I. Now I have told you before it happened so that when it comes to pass you may believe. I will not talk much more with you, for the prince of this world is coming, and he will have nothing in me, but that the world may know that I love the Father, and just as my Father commanded me, this I do.

Arise, let us go hence.

Section 160. DISCOURSE OF JESUS ON THE WAY TO GETHSEMANE

Mark 14:26. Matthew 26:30. Luke 22:39. John 15 and 16

When they had sung a hymn, he went out, as his custom was, to the Mount of Olives; the disciples also followed him.

[As they went, he said] I am the true vine, and my Father is the husbandman. He takes away every vine in me that stops bearing fruit and repeatedly prunes every vine which bears fruit to make it bear more fruit. You are already clean because of the word which I have spoken to you. Abide in me, and I will abide in you. Just as no branch can of itself bear fruit unless it continues to abide in the vine, neither can you unless you continue to abide in me. I am the vine; you are the branches. He who continues to abide in me and I in him, he will bear much fruit, for without me you can do nothing. If anyone does not continue to abide in me, he will be thrown out as the branch, and after it withers, men gather it up and cast it into the fire to burn. If you continue to abide in me and my words continue to abide in you, ask what you wish, and it shall come to you. In this is my Father glorified: that you bear much fruit and be my disciples.

As my Father loved me, so also have I loved you. Abide in my love. If you will continue to keep my commandments, you will abide in my love; just as I have kept my Father's commandments and abide in his love. These things have I spoken to you that my joy may be in you and that your joy may be complete. This is my commandment that you love one another just as I have loved you. Greater love than this has no man, that one lay down his life for his friend. You are my friends if you keep on doing what I command you. No longer do I call you slaves because the slave does not know what his master does. I have called you friends because all things which I have heard from my Father, I have made known to you. You have not chosen me; I have chosen you and appointed you to go and bear fruit and have your fruit abide. So whatever you ask the Father in my name, he will give you. These things I command you, that you love one another.

If the world continues to hate you, you know that it has hated me before you. If you were of the world, the world would love its own. Because you are not of the world, but I have chosen you out of the world, the world continues to hate you. Remember the word which I said to you, The slave is not greater than his master. If they have persecuted me, they will persecute you also. If they have kept my word, they will keep yours too. All these things they will do to you on account of my name, because they have not known him who sent me. If I had not come and spoken to them, they would have had no sin. Now they have no excuse for their sin. He who continues to hate me continues to hate my Father also. If I had not done the works among them which no one else ever did, they would have had no sin. Now they have seen and hated both me and my Father. This is so the word in the Law might be fulfilled where it is written:

They hated me without cause.

When the Helper comes, whom I send to you from my Father, the Spirit of Truth which goes out from the Father, he will testify of me. You also will testify, for you were with me from the beginning.

These things have I spoken to you lest you be made to stumble. They will put you out of the synagogues; yes, the hour comes when everyone who kills you will think that he does service to God. They will do this because they have not known the Father nor me. These things have I told you that when their hour comes, you may remember that I told you of them. I have not told you these things from the first, because I was with you. Now I go away to him who sent me, and none of you asks, Where do you go? But because I have spoken these things to you, sorrow has filled your hearts. I tell you the truth, it is best for you that I go away. If I went not away, the Helper would not come to you. But if I go, I will send him to you. *through fellowship of the church.*

He, when he comes, will convict the world of sin and of righteousness and of judgment: of sin, because they do not believe on me; of righteousness, because I go to the Father and you see me no longer; and of judgment, because the prince of the world has been judged.

I still have many things to tell you, but you are not able to bear them now. When he, the Spirit of Truth, is come, he will guide you into all truth. He will not speak from himself; he will speak whatever he hears. He will declare to you the coming things. He will glorify me, for he will receive from me and declare to you. All things that the Father has are mine. Therefore I said to you, He receives from me and declares to you.

Yet a little while and you will see me no more; again after a little you will see me.

His disciples said to one another, What is this which he speaks to us, A little while and you will not see me; again a little while and you will see me? and, I go to the Father?

They said, What is this little while that he speaks of? We do not know what he means.

Jesus knew that they wished to ask him, so he said to them, Do you inquire among yourselves about my saying, A little while and you will not see me; and again a little while and you will see me? Truly, truly, I say to you that you will weep and mourn, but the world will rejoice. You will be filled with sorrow, but your sorrow will turn to rejoicing. The woman has anguish when she gives birth because her hour has come; but when the child is born, she no longer remembers the anguish because of the joy that a child is born into the world. Likewise you also have sorrow now. You will see me again, and your hearts will rejoice, and no man will take away your joy from you. In that day you will ask me nothing. Truly, truly, I tell you, whatever you ask the Father, he will give to you in my name. Up to now you have asked nothing in my name. Ask and you will receive that your joy may be complete.

These things have I spoken to you by proverbs. The hour comes when I will no longer speak to you in proverbs, but will tell you plainly about the Father. In that day you shall ask in my name, and I do not promise that I will ask the Father for you; the Father himself loves you because you have loved me and believed that I came from God. I came from the Father and I have come into the world. Again I leave the world and go to the Father.

His disciples were saying, Lo, now you speak plainly and tell us no proverb. Now we know that you know all things and have no need that anyone should ask you. Thus we believe that you came from God.

Jesus answered them, Do you believe now? Lo, the hour comes, yes, it has come, that each of you will be scattered and leave me alone. Yet, I am not alone, for the Father is with me. These things have I spoken to you so you may have peace in me. In the world you will have tribulation. But be of good cheer, I have overcome the world.

Section 161. The Prayer of Jesus

John 17

Jesus spoke these things; then, lifting his eyes to heaven, he said, Father, the hour has come. Glorify thy Son that the Son may glorify thee, just as thou hast given him authority over all flesh that he may give eternal life to all whom thou hast given him. This is eternal life, that they know thee, the only true God, and Jesus the Messiah whom thou hast sent. I have glorified thee upon the earth by completing the work which thou didst give me to do. Now, Father, Glorify thou me in thy presence with the glory which I had with thee before the world came to be. I have revealed thy name to the men whom thou didst give me out of the world. They were thine, and thou gavest them to me, and they have kept thy word. Now they know that everything which thou gavest me is from thee. For the words which thou gavest me, I have given to them, and they received them, and knew of a truth that I came from thee, and they believed that thou didst send me.

I pray for them. I do not pray for the world, but for them whom thou gavest me, for they are thine (and all that are mine are thine, and thine are mine), and I have been glorified in them. I am no longer in the world, but these are in the world; I come to thee. Holy Father, keep them in thy name which thou hast given me, that they may be one just as we are one. When I was with them, I kept them in thy name which thou gavest me: I guarded them, and not one of them perished—only the son of destruction that the scripture might be fulfilled. But now I come to thee, and I speak these things in the world that they might have my joy complete in themselves. I have given them thy word, and the world has hated them because they do not belong to the world just as I do not belong to the world. I do not ask that thou shouldest take them out of the world, but that thou wilt keep them from the Evil One. They do not belong to the world just as I do not belong to the world. Consecrate them through the truth. Thy word is truth. Just as thou didst send me into the world, I also have sent them into the world. I consecrate myself for them that they may also be consecrated in truth.

I do not pray for these only, but also for those who are to believe in me through their word; may they all be one! As thou, Father, art in me and I in thee; may they also be in us!—that the world may believe that thou didst send me. I have given them the glory which thou didst give me that they may be one just as we are one, I in them and thou in me, that they may be perfectly one, so that the world may know that thou didst send me and that thou lovest them just as thou didst love me.

Father, what thou didst give me, I desire that they may be with me where I am to see my glory which thou didst give me, for thou didst love me before the foundation of the world. Righteous Father, the world has not known thee, but I have known thee, and these have known that thou didst send me. I have made thy name known to them and will make it known, that the love with which thou lovest me may be in them, and I in them.

Section 162. JESUS IN GETHSEMANE

Mark 14:32-42. Matthew 26:36-46.
Luke 22:40-46. John 18:1

When Jesus had spoken these things, he came with his disciples across the Kidron Brook, and he and his disciples entered into a garden which was there. The name of the place is Gethsemane. He said to the disciples, You sit here while I go yonder and pray. Pray that you may not be overcome by temptation.

Taking Peter and James and John with him, he began to be sorrowful and bewildered, He said to them, My soul is crushed with sorrow even unto death. Stay here and watch with me.

He went forward a little, about a stone's throw, and fell down upon the ground and prayed that if it were possible the hour might pass away from him. He said, Abba (Father), all things are possible with thee. If it is possible, take this cup from me. Nevertheless, not my will, but thine be done.

There appeared to him an angel from heaven strengthening him. Being in agony, he prayed more earnestly. His sweat became as clots of blood falling upon the earth.[4]

He arose from his praying and came to his disciples and found them sleeping. He said to Peter, Simon, are you sleeping? What! Could you not watch with me one hour? Rise up! Watch and pray lest you enter into temptation. The spirit indeed is willing, but the flesh is weak.

Again, a second time, he went and prayed, saying, My Father, if it is impossible for this to pass away except I drink it, thy will be done.

Coming again, he found them sleeping, for their eyes were heavy; and they did not know what to answer him.

So, leaving them, he went away and prayed the same thing again.

He came to the disciples a third time and said to them' Are you still sleeping and taking your rest? Enough of this! Lo, the hour has come, and the Son of man is delivered into the hands of sinners. Arise! Let us go. Lo, he that betrays me is near.

4. The textual evidence is about evenly divided for and against this reading. It is with considerable questioning that I leave it in the text, but, as yet, the evidence is not strong enough to relegate this to the margin.

CHAPTER XVI

A RANSOM FOR MANY

Section 163. BETRAYED, ARRESTED, AND FORSAKEN

Mark 14:43-52.   Matthew 26:47-56.
Luke 22:47-53.   John 18:2-12

Judas, the betrayer, being one of the twelve, knew the place, for Jesus frequently came there with his disciples.   While Jesus was still speaking, he came with a great crowd of soldiers and officers from the chief priests, scribes, elders, and the Pharisees carrying staves and swords with lanterns and torches.

Now the betrayer had given them a sign, saying, Whom I kiss, that one is he.   Lay hold on him and lead him safely away. So he came to Jesus and said, Hail, Rabbi.   Then he kissed him.

Jesus said to him, Judas, do you betray the Son of man with a kiss?

Knowing that all things were come upon him, Jesus went and said to them, Whom do you seek?

They answered, Jesus of Nazareth.

He said, I am he.

When he said, I am he, they went backward and fell to the ground.

Again he asked them, Whom do you seek?

They said, Jesus of Nazareth.

Jesus answered, I told you that I am he.   If therefore you seek me, let these go away.

[This he said] that the word might be fulfilled which he spoke:

Whom thou hast given me,
I have not lost one of them.

They came and laid hands on Jesus and took him. And those with him, seeing, said, Lord, shall we strike with the sword?

One of them, Simon Peter, having a sword, stretched out his hand, drew his sword, struck the slave of the high priest, and cut off his right ear. The name of the slave was Malchus.

Jesus said, Suffer this much. And touching the ear, he healed it.

He said to Peter, Put your sword in its place. All who take the sword shall die by the sword. Or, do you not know that I could pray my Father and he would send more than twelve legions of angels? The cup which my Father gave me, shall I not drink it? How then would the Scriptures be fulfilled that thus it must be?

Jesus said to the chief priests and the officers of the temple and the elders who had come out against him, Do you come as upon a robber with swords and staves to take me? When I sat daily with you in the temple teaching, you did not stretch out your hand against me. But this is your hour and the authority of darkness. This has all happened that the writings of the prophets might be fulfilled.

Then the band, and the chief captain and the officers of the Jews took Jesus and bound him.

All the disciples left him and fled.

A certain young man followed him with a linen cloth wrapped around his naked body, and they laid hold on him. But leaving the linen cloth, he fled naked.

Section 164. PRELIMINARY HEARING BEFORE ANNAS

John 18:13-14, 19-23

They led him first to Annas. He was the father-in-law of Caiaphas, who was high priest that year. Caiaphas was the one who advised the Jews that it was expedient for one man to die for the people. Therefore the high priest asked Jesus about his disciples and his doctrine.

Jesus answered him, I have spoken openly in the world. I have always taught in the synagogue and in the temple where all the Jews gather together, and nothing have I spoken in secret. Why do you ask me? Ask those who heard what I spoke to them, Lo, they know what I said.

As he spoke these things, one of the officers who stood by struck Jesus a blow, saying, Do you answer the high priest so?

Jesus answered him, If I have spoken evil, testify concerning the evil; but if well, why did you strike me?

Section 165. TRIAL BY CAIAPHAS AND THE SANHEDRIN

Mark 14:53, 55-65.   Matthew 26:57, 59-68.
Luke 22:54, 63-65.   John 18:24

Annas sent him away bound, to Caiaphas, the high priest. Those who had arrested him led Jesus away to the house of Caiaphas, the high priest; all the chief priests and the elders and the scribes came together with him.

The high priest and the whole council kept seeking false witnesses against Jesus that they might put him to death. But they found none. For though many false witnesses came forward, their testimony did not agree together. Afterward there came two false witnesses against him, saying, This one said, and we hear him say, I am able to destroy this temple of God which is made with hands and in three days raise another made without hands.

But not even in this did their testimony agree.

The high priest stood in their midst and asked Jesus, Do you answer nothing to this testimony against you?

Jesus kept silent and answered not at all.

Again the high priest asked him, Are you the Messiah, the Son of the blessed God? I adjure you by the living God, tell us.

Jesus said to them, I am he. Moreover, hereafter, you will see the Son of man sitting at the right hand of Power and coming on the clouds of heaven.

The high priest tore his robes, saying, He has blasphemed. Why do we still need witnesses? Lo, you have heard the blasphemy; what is your verdict?

They all condemned him to be worthy of death.

The men who held him began to beat him and mock him and spit in his face. They blindfolded him, saying, Prophesy to us, you Messiah, who was it that struck you? And many other things they spoke against him, reviling him. The officers received him with blows.

Section 166. PETER DENIES HIS LORD

Mark 14:54, 66-72.   Matthew 26:58, 69-75.
Luke 22:54-62.   John 18:15-18, 25-27.

Simon Peter had followed him at a distance, as did another disciple.[1] That disciple was known to the high priest, and he entered in with Jesus to the courtyard of the high priest But Peter stood outside by the door. Therefore that other disciple who was known to the high priest came out and spoke to the door-keeper and brought Peter into the court of the high priest.

The slaves and officers, having kindled a fire of charcoal in the midst of the court, were sitting there together, for it was cold. Peter sat down among them to see the end and warmed himself by the fire.

---

1. All the evangelists record three denials by Peter during the course of the three Jewish trials, which covered a period of about six hours. Details do not match, so some editing and rearrangement has been necessary to achieve a blended account. The above is an account that contains an order of events that might well have happened without any claim for infallibility.

While Peter was there in the court, warming himself by the fire, one of the maids of the high priest came and saw Peter. She looked intently at him and said, You too were with Jesus of Nazareth which is in Galilee.

They said therefore to him, Are you also one of his disciples?

He denied it and said, I am not.   I neither know nor understand what you say.   Woman, I do not know him.

He went out on the porch and the cock crew.   There another maid saw him, she who kept the door, and said to them that were there, This man too was with Jesus the Nazarene.

Again he denied it, saying, I am not.   With an oath, he said, I do not know the man.

After about an hour, one of the slaves of the high priest, being a kinsman of him whose ear Peter had cut off, said, Did not I see you in the garden with him?   He began confidently to affirm, Of a truth this one was with him.   He is a Galilean for his dialect gives him away.

Then he began to curse and to swear, I do not know this man of whom you speak.

The cock crew at once a second time; the Lord turned around and looked at Peter; then Peter remembered the word which Jesus had spoken to him, Before the cock crows twice, you will deny me three times.   So, going outside, he began to weep bitterly.

Section 167. FORMAL TRIAL BY THE SANHEDRIN

Mark 15:1.   Matthew 27:1.   Luke 22:66-71

In the morning as soon as day came, the council of the people —elders, chief priests, and scribes—held a consultation against Jesus to put him to death.   They brought him back to their Sanhedrin, saying, If you are the Messiah, tell us.

He said to them, If I tell you, you will not believe.   If I question you, you will not answer.   From now on the Son of man will be sitting at the right hand of the power of God.

They all said, Are you the Son of God?

He said to them, You say that I am.

They said, Why do we still need testimony?   We ourselves have heard from his own mouth.

Section 168. The Suicide of Judas

Matthew 27: 3-10

When Judas, his betrayer, saw that he was condemned, he regretted his action and returned the thirty pieces of silver to the chief priests and elders, saying, I sinned when I betrayed innocent blood.

They said, What is that to us?   You see to it.

Throwing the money down in the sanctuary, he went out and hanged himself.

The chief priests took the money and said, It is not lawful to put it into the sacred treasury since it is the price of blood.

So they consulted and took the money and bought the potter's field with it to bury strangers in.   Therefore, that field is called, The field of blood, to this day.

Then was fulfilled the word of Jeremiah the prophet who said:

> They took the thirty pieces of silver—
> The price of him who was priced,
> Whom the sons of Israel priced—
> And gave them for the potter's field just as the Lord
>   directed me.

Section 169. The First Trial Before Pilate

Mark 15:1-5.   Matthew 27:2, 11-14.
Luke 23:1-5.   John 18:28-38

The whole company rose up to bring him before Pilate. They bound him and led him from Caiaphas to the palace, to Pilate the governor, and it was early.   They themselves entered not into the palace, that they might not be defiled, but might eat the Passover.   Therefore Pilate came out to them and said, What accusation do you bring against this man?

They answered, If this one were not a criminal, we would not have brought him to you.

Pilate said to them, Take him yourselves, and judge him by your law.

The Jews said to him, It is not legal for us to put anyone to death.

[This they said] that the word of Jesus might be fulfilled when he spoke concerning the manner of his death.

They began to accuse him, We found this man perverting our nation, forbidding the payment of taxes to Caesar, and claiming that he is the Messiah, a king.

Pilate went into the palace again, called Jesus, and asked him, Are you the king of the Jews?

Jesus answered, Do you speak of yourself or did another tell you of me?

Pilate answered, Am I a Jew?   Your own people and the chief priests have delivered you to me.   What have you done?

Jesus answered, My kingdom is not of this world.   If my kingdom were of this world, my officers would fight to keep me from being delivered to the Jews.   But now my kingdom is not from here.

Pilate said to him, Are you a king then?

Jesus answered, You say that I am a king. I was begotten and came into the world for this, that I might testify to the truth. Everyone who is of the truth hears my voice.

Pilate said to him, What is truth?

Having said this, Pilate went out to the Jews and said to them, I find no crime in this man.

The chief priests and the elders began to accuse him much.

Pilate again asked, Do you answer nothing? Behold how many things they accuse you of.

Jesus did not answer him to so much as a word. Pilate marveled greatly. Then Pilate spoke to the chief priests and to the crowds, I find no crime in this man.

They were the more urgent, saying, He stirs up the people of all Judea beginning from Galilee even to this place.

Section 170. BACK AND FORTH TO HEROD

Luke 23:6-12

When Pilate heard this, he asked if the man were a Galilean. When he knew that he was under the jurisdiction of Herod, he sent him to Herod who was himself in Jerusalem in these days.

Herod was delighted to see him, for he had wished for a long time to see him; he had heard of him and was hoping to see a sign done by him. He questioned him with many words.

But Jesus answered him nothing.

The chief priests and the scribes were standing by and accusing him vigorously.

Herod with his soldiers, after treating him with contempt and mocking him, put a bright robe on him and sent him back to Pilate. Herod and Pilate became friends with one another on that day, for previously they had been at enmity with one another.

Section 171. JESUS BEFORE PILATE AGAIN

Mark 15:6-19.   Matthew 27:15-30.
Luke 23:13-25.   John 18:39 to 19:16

The governor's custom was to release one prisoner during the feast, whom the people chose. He had a notable prisoner named Barrabas lying bound with those who had made insurrection, men who in the insurrection had done murder. The people went up and began to ask him to do this for them.

Pilate therefore called the chief priests and the rulers and people and said to them, You brought this man to me as one who perverts the people. Lo, I have examined him before you and found none of the crimes in him of which you accuse him. No, nor did Herod. For he sent him back to us. Behold, he has done nothing worthy of death. You have a custom that I should release someone to you during the Passover. Whom do you want me to release, Barabbas or Jesus, who is called the Messiah? I will chastise and release to you the king of the Jews.

He knew that the chief priests had delivered him through jealousy. Besides, his wife had sent to him while he was sitting on the judgment seat, saying, Have nothing to do with this righteous man, for I have suffered many things today in a dream because of him.

The chief priests and the elders, however, persuaded the people to ask for Barabbas and destroy Jesus.

Pilate asked them again, Which of them do you wish me to release to you? Him whom you call the king of the Jews?

They all cried out, Not this man but Barabbas.

Pilate said, What then shall I do with Jesus which is called the Messiah?

They all said, Crucify him, crucify him!

Pilate spoke again to them, wishing to release Jesus!

They all replied, Away with this man. Release Barabbas to us.

He said for the third time, What evil has this man done? I have found nothing in him worthy of death. I will chastise him and let him go.

But they cried out exceedingly, Let him be crucified.

Pilate took Jesus and scourged him. The soldiers of the governor took Jesus into the court of the palace and called the whole band together. They stripped him and put a scarlet robe on him. They plaited a crown of thorns and put it on his head, and a reed in his right hand. Then, bowing the knees before him, they mocked him, saying, Hail, King of the Jews! They spit on him, slapped him, and took the reed and struck him on the head.[2]

Then Pilate came out again and said to them, Behold I bring him out to you in order that you may know that I find no crime in him.

Jesus came out, wearing the crown of thorns and the scarlet robe. He said to them, Behold, the man.

When they saw him, the chief priests and officers, cried out, Crucify him! Crucify him!

Pilate said, You take him and crucify him. I find no crime in him.

The Jews answered, We have a law; by our law he ought to die, for he made himself the Son of God.

When Pilate heard this word, he was the more afraid, so he came again into the palace and said to Jesus, Where are you from?

Jesus gave him no answer.

---

2. Matthew and Mark give this mocking after the condemnation. John's account, however, seems more true to the circumstances. Pilate used it to try to effect a compromise and avoid the necessity of condemning Jesus.

Pilate said to him, Do you not speak to me? Do you not know that I have authority to release you and authority to crucify you?

Jesus answered, You have no authority over me except what has been given you from above. Therefore, he who betrays me has greater sin than you.

Therefore, Pilate sought to release him.

But the Jews cried out, If you release this man, you are no friend to Caesar. Everyone who makes himself a king is Caesar's enemy.

When Pilate heard these words, he brought Jesus out and sat down upon the judgment seat at the place called, The Pavement, but in Hebrew, Babbatha.

It was the preparation during the Passover; it was about six o'clock.[3]

Pilate said to the Jews, Behold your king.

But they were instant with loud voices and cried out, Away with him! Away with him! Crucify him!

Pilate said to them, Shall I crucify your king?

The chief priests answered, We have no king but Caesar.

When Pilate saw that he could not prevail, but rather a tumult was raised, he took water and washed his hands before the multitude, saying, I am innocent of this blood. You see to it.

The people said, His blood be upon us and upon our children.

Pilate, wishing to please the people, gave sentence that their request should be granted. So he released him who for insurrection and murder had been cast into prison—Barabbas. But Jesus, he scourged and delivered to be crucified.

---

3. A. T. Robertson, *Harmony*, 284–287, concludes that John reckons time by the Roman system. Thus the sixth hour would be six o'clock in the morning. Other accounts agree that Jesus was put on the cross at nine o'clock. So this conclusion is sustained by the facts of the case. This same system of time may have been used by John in previous mentions of time, but this is the only place where a question of harmony arises.

Section 172. Jesus on the Way to Golgotha

Mark 15:20-23.   Matthew 27:31-34.
Luke 23:26-33.   John 19:16,17

When they had mocked him, they took off the scarlet robe, clothed him in his own garments, and led him out to be crucified. Jesus went out therefore bearing his cross.

As they led him away, they found a man of Cyrene, named Simon, coming from the country, the father of Alexander and Rufus. Him they compelled to go with them and carry the cross after Jesus.

A great multitude of people followed him, and women who wept for him and mourned over him. Jesus turned to them and said, You daughters of Jerusalem, Stop weeping over me; weep rather for yourselves and for your children. For, a time is coming when they will say, Blessed are the barren and the wombs which never gave birth and the breasts that never gave suck. Then will they begin to say to the mountains, Fall upon us, and to the hills, Cover us. If they do these things in the green tree, what shall be done to the dry?

They also led two others with him to be put to death who were criminals.

When they came to a place called Golgotha in the Hebrew, the place of the skull, they gave him wine to drink mingled with gall. He, having tasted it, would not drink.

Section 173. The First Three Hours on the Cross

Mark 15:24-32.   Matthew 27:35-44.   Luke 23:33-43.
John 19:18-27

It was nine o'clock when they crucified him, and with him the two criminals, one on his right hand and the other on his left.

Jesus said, Father, forgive them, for they know not what they do.[4]

Pilate wrote a title and placed it on the cross over his head. This was his accusation. On it was written: JESUS OF NAZARETH, THE KING OF THE JEWS. This title many of the Jews read, for the place where Jesus was crucified was near the city, and it was written in Hebrew, Latin, and Greek.

The chief priests kept saying to Pilate, Do not write, The king of the Jews, but, that he said, I am king of the Jews.

Pilate answered, What I have written stands written.

The soldiers, when they had crucified Jesus, took his garments and made four parts, to each soldier a part, and the cloke. The cloke was without seam, woven throughout. They said therefore to one another, Let us not cut it but cast lots whose it shall be. That the scripture might be fulfilled:

They parted my garments among them,
And for my cloke they cast lots.

The soldiers, therefore, did these things. Then they sat there and watched him.

The people stood, beholding, and they who passed by insulted him, wagging their heads and saying, You who destroy the temple and rebuild it in three days, come down from the cross and save yourself if you are the Son of God.

In like manner the chief priests and elders scoffed among themselves and with the rulers and scribes, saying, He saved others; he cannot save himself. If this is the Messiah of God, the elect, the king of Israel, let him come down from the cross that we may see and believe on him. He trusted God, let him deliver him now if he will. For he said, I am the Son of God.

---

4. Some of the oldest and best manuscripts do not have this verse, and Westcott and Hort bracket it. However, the uncertainty as to whether these words are a genuine part of Luke's Gospel does not extend to whether they were spoken by Jesus or not. They are too much like him and too utterly unlike anyone else not to be genuine.

The soldiers also mocked him, going to him, and offering him vinegar, saying, If you are the king of the Jews, save yourself.

The robbers also that were crucified with him cast the same reproach at him. One of the criminals railed on him, saying, Are you not the Messiah? Save yourself and us.

The other rebuked him and said, Do you not fear God, seeing that you are in the same condemnation? We indeed justly, for we have done things worthy of condemnation. But he has done nothing wrong.

Then he said, Jesus, remember me when you come into your kingdom.

Jesus answered him, Truly, I say to you, today you will be with me in paradise.

There was standing by the cross of Jesus his mother and his mother's sister, Mary the wife of Cleopas, and Mary Magdalene. When Jesus saw his mother and that disciple whom he loved standing by, he said to his mother, Woman, behold your son. Then he said to the disciple, Behold your mother. From that hour the disciple took her into his own house.

Section 174. THREE HOURS OF DARKNESS

Mark 15:33-37.   Matthew 27:45-50.   Luke 23:44-45a,46
John 19:28-30

About noon a darkness came over the whole earth until three o'clock, the sun failing to shine. At three o'clock, Jesus cried out with a loud voice, Eloi, Eloi, Lama, Sabackthani? (that is, My God, my God, why hast thou forsaken me?)

Some of them standing by, heard him. They said, Behold he calls for Elijah.

After this, Jesus, knowing that all things were already completed that the scripture might be fulfilled, said, I thirst

There was set there a vessel full of sour wine, so one of them ran and took a sponge and filled it with sour wine, put it on a reed, and brought it to his mouth for him to drink. The rest said, Let him be, let's see if Elijah comes to save him.

When he had received the wine, Jesus said, It is finished.

Then he cried out with a great voice, Father into thy hands I commend my spirit. Having said this, he gave up the spirit.

Section 175. Wonders Accompanying the Crucifixion

Mark 15:38-41.   Matthew 27:51-56.   Luke 23:45b, 47-49

Lo, the veil of the temple was rent in two from the top to the bottom, the earth quaked, the rocks were rent, and the graves were opened, and many of the bodies of the saints that slept were raised. Coming out of the tombs after his resurrection, they went into the Holy City and appeared to many.

When the centurion and those with him watching Jesus saw the earthquake and the things that were done, they were greatly afraid and said, Truly, this is a son of God. He was innocent. And he glorified God.

All the multitudes that came together to see this, seeing the things that were done, returned, smiting their breasts.

There were women there watching from afar who had followed with him from Galilee, serving him. Among them were Mary Magdalene, Mary the mother of James the less and Joses and Salome, the mother of the sons of Zebedee, and many others who came with him to Jerusalem.

Section 176. The Burial of Jesus

Mark 15:42-46.   Matthew 27:57-60.   Luke 23:50-54.
John 19:31-42

Since it was Preparation, that the bodies might not remain on the cross during the sabbath, for that sabbath was a great day, the Jews asked Pilate that their legs might be broken and that they might be taken away.

The soldiers came and broke the legs of the first and of the other who had been crucified with him. But upon coming to Jesus, they saw that he was already dead, so they did not break his legs; but one of the soldiers pierced his side with a spear, and blood and water came out at once. He that saw has given testimony, and his testimony is true, and he knows that he tells the truth, that you also may believe. For these things happened in order that the scripture might be fulfilled:

His bones have they not broken.

Again another scripture says:

They shall look on him whom they pierced.

Evening having come, Joseph of Arimathaea, a member of the council, a good man and upright (he had not consented to their counsel and deed), who was looking for the kingdom of God and was a disciple of Jesus (but secretly for fear of the Jews), went to Pilate and asked that he might take away the body of Jesus. Pilate marveled that he was already dead, and calling the centurion, he asked him if he had been dead for some time. When he learned it from the centurion, he ordered the body given to Joseph.

He came and took it away. Nicodemus also came, he who came to him by night at first, bearing a mixture of myrrh and aloes about a hundred pounds. They took down the body of Jesus and wrapped it in a clean linen cloth with the spices as the custom of the Jews is in burying. In the place where he was crucified, there was a garden, and in the garden Joseph owned a new tomb hewn out of rock in which no man had ever been laid. There they laid him, for it was near by, it being the Preparation of the Jews and the sabbath drawing on. They also rolled a great stone against the door of the tomb, then they went away.

Section 177. The Watch of the Women by the Tomb

Mark 15:47.   Matthew 27:61-66.   Luke 23:55-56

The women which had come with him out of Galilee followed and saw the tomb where his body was laid. There, Mary Magdalene and the other Mary, the Mother of Joses, sat in front of the tomb.

[The rest] returned and prepared spices and ointments. But on the sabbath they rested according to the commandment.

On the morrow, the day after the Preparation, the chief priests and the Pharisees came to Pilate, saying, Sir, we remember that that deceiver said while still living, After three days I will rise again.   Give orders therefore to make the tomb secure until the three days, lest the disciples coming, steal him and say to the people, He was risen from the dead: the last error would be worse than the first.

Pilate said to them, You have a guard; go and make it as secure as you know how.

They went therefore and made the tomb secure, sealing the stone and setting a guard.

CHAPTER XVII

THE LIVING SAVIOUR

Section 178. THE WOMEN MAKE PREPARATION TO ANOINT JESUS

Mark 16:1.   Matthew 28:1

Late on the sabbath, while the first day of the week was drawing on, Mary Magdalene and Mary the mother of James and Salome came to see the tomb.

As soon as the sabbath was over, they (were planning) to bring spices to anoint him.

Section 179. THE RESURRECTION

Matthew 28:2-4

Lo, there was a great earthquake, for an angel of the Lord descended from heaven and came and rolled away the stone and sat upon it; his appearance was as lightning and his clothes were white as snow.   For fear of him, the guards trembled and became as dead men.

Section 180. VISIT OF MARY MAGDALENE TO THE TOMB

John 20:1-2a

While it was yet dark, Mary Magdalene came to the tomb. She saw the stone taken away from the tomb and ran to Simon Peter and the other disciple whom Jesus loved.

Section 181. THE VISIT OF OTHER WOMEN TO THE TOMB

Mark 16:2-7. Matthew 28:5-8. Luke 24:1-8

Just as the sun rose, (the other women) came to the tomb bringing the spices which they had prepared.[1]

They kept saying to one another, Who will roll away the stone from the door for us?

But when they looked up, they saw that the stone had been rolled away, for it was very great.

They entered into the tomb but they did not find the body of the Lord Jesus.

As they were perplexed concerning this, lo, two men stood by them in dazzling apparel. They were terrified and bowed their faces to the earth.

The angel said to the women, Be not afraid. I know that you seek Jesus of Nazareth who was crucified. He is risen. He is not here. Why seek the living among the dead? Remember how he spoke to you while he was still in Galilee, saying, The Son of man must be delivered up into the hands of sinful

---

1. These sections comprise the climax of the Gospel accounts. The exact order of the happenings in the early hours of the first day of the week is very difficult to reconstruct. In the final analysis, each student must decide for himself just when each recorded event happened. The arrangement we have made seems logical and does not violate the reliability of any account. When we remember the many things that did happen and the scarcity of our material about it, we need not wonder that the story is not altogether clear. It is implied in the accounts that a number of pious women kept watch at the tomb of Jesus from the moment of his burial till the early hours of Sunday. It seems that as soon as the shops opened at 6 o'clock on Saturday night, the Jewish sabbath ending at that time, the women bought the spices in preparation for an early trip to the tomb to anoint the body of Jesus. No doubt a large group of women were planning this early pilgrimage. It seems, however, from John's account that Mary Magdalene came first to the tomb and found it empty. She immediately ran to tell Peter and John. While she was gone, the other women seem to have arrived and seen the vision of angels. Some of them went at once to tell the disciples, while others fled in superstitious fear and said nothing. While they were on their way, Peter and John came to the tomb and after seeing it, returned to the city. It is not clear whether they arrived in time to hear the report of the women who had visited the tomb to the disciples. Probably not. Mary Magdalene seems to have followed Peter and John back to the tomb, reaching it after they left, and to have been the first to see the risen Lord. After the women made their report to the disciples, they naturally returned to the tomb. On the way, Jesus appeared to them. After this, the order of events is clear if we accept the accounts as given. We must remember that the main thing is not a reliable chronology of events on the ressurection morning, but the assurance of the resurrection. This very diversity in witnesses gives strength to their testimony that the resurrection did occur.

men and be crucified and on the third day rise again. Come now and see the place where he lay. (Then they remembered his words.) Go quickly and tell his disciples and Peter that he is risen from the dead, and, lo, he goes before you into Galilee. There, you will see him just as he told you. Behold, I have told you.

Section 182. THE WOMEN DIVIDE AND RETURN TO THE CITY

Mark 16:8. Matthew 28:9. Luke 24:9-11

[Some of them] went out and fled from the tomb; trembling and astonishment had come upon them, and they told nothing to anyone, for they were afraid.

[The others] went away quickly from the tomb with fear and great joy and ran to tell the disciples. Joanna, Mary the mother of James, Mary Magdalene,[2] and the other women with them told all these things to the eleven and to all the rest But the story seemed to them to be empty talk and they would not believe them.

Section 183. PETER AND JOHN VISIT THE TOMB

John 20:2-10

(When Mary Magdalene came to Peter and the other disciple), she said to them, They have taken the Lord out of the tomb, and we do not know where they put him.

Then Peter and the other disciple came out and went toward the tomb. They were both running together, but the other disciple outran Peter and came first to the tomb. He stooped down and saw the linen cloths lying there, but he did not go in. Simon Peter came, following him, and he went into the tomb.

---

2. Luke mentions Mary Magdalene as coming with the other women to all the disciples. However, he does not mention the special incidents recorded by John. His record may be regarded as a summary of all that took place on that eventful morning. Thus, there is no necessary contradiction to John's record, since Mary Magdalene did have a part in informing the disciples of the empty grave.

He saw the linen cloths lying, and the napkin which was upon his head, not lying with the linen cloths but apart, rolled up in a place by itself. Then the other disciple who came first to the tomb, came in, saw, and believed. For they did not yet understand the scriptures that he must arise from the dead.

The disciples went back again to their home.

Section 184. Jesus Appears to Mary Magdalene

John 20:11-18

Meanwhile Mary stood by the tomb weeping. As she wept she stooped and looked into the tomb, and she saw two angels in white clothing, sitting—one at the head, the other at the feet—where the body of Jesus had been lying. They said to her, Woman why do you weep?

She said to them, Because they have taken away my Lord and I know not where they have laid him.

When she had spoken these things, she turned around and saw Jesus standing behind her. She did not know that it was Jesus. Jesus said to her, Woman, why are you weeping? Whom do you seek?

She, thinking he was the gardener, said to him, Sir, if you have carried him away, tell me where you laid him, and I will take him away.

Jesus said to her, Mary

She, turning, said to him in Hebrew, Rabboni (which means, Teacher).

Jesus said to her, Cling not to me for I have not yet ascended to the Father. Go to my brothers and say to them, I ascend to my Father and your Father and to my God and your God.

Then Mary Magdalene came and reported to the disciples, I have seen the Lord and he told me these things.

Section 185. JESUS APPEARS TO THE WOMEN

Matthew 28:9-10

[As the women returned to the tomb], Lo, Jesus met them saying, Hail!

They came up to him and took hold of his feet and worshipped him.

Jesus said to them, Be not afraid; go tell my brothers to go away into Galilee and there they will see me.

Section 186. THE REPORT OF THE GUARD

Matthew 28:11-15

While they were going, behold, some of the guard came into the city and reported to the chief priests all the things that had happened. When they had assembled with the elders and taken counsel, they gave the soldiers much money, saying, You tell it that his disciples came by night and stole him while you were sleeping. If anyone reports this to the governor, we will persuade him and you will have no worry.

They took the money and did as they had been directed.

Therefore this story is told among the Jews to this day.

Section 187. JESUS APPEARS TO THE TWO DISCIPLES ON THE ROAD TO EMMAUS

Luke 24:13-35

Lo, on that very day two of them were going to a village named Emmaus about seven miles from Jerusalem, and they were talking with one another about all these things that had happened. While they were talking together and questioning, Jesus himself drew near and began to go along with them. But their eyes were prevented from recognizing him.

He said to them, What are these words which you are exchanging with one another as you walk?

They stopped with puzzled countenances. One of them named Cleopas said to him, Are you the only visitor to Jerusalem who does not know what has happened there in these days?

He said to them, What things?

They said to him, Those which concern Jesus of Nazareth who became a prophet mighty in word and deed before God and all the people, how the chief priests and our rulers delivered him to the condemnation of death and they crucified him. We had hoped that he was the coming redeemer of Israel. Yes, and besides this, it is the third day since these things happened. Also certain women among us amazed us. For after going to the tomb early and not finding the body, they came claiming to have seen a vision of angels who said that he was alive. Some of us went out with them to the tomb, and found it just as the women said, but we did not find him.

He said, O foolish men and slow of heart to believe all that the prophets have spoken. Was it not necessary for the Messiah to suffer and so to enter into his glory? Then beginning with Moses and all the prophets, he explained to them in all the scriptures the things which concerned himself.

They drew near to the village where they were going, and he acted as though he would go on farther. But they invited him earnestly, saying, Stay with us, for it is toward evening and the day is nearly gone.

He entered in to stay with them. When he broke bread with them, he took the bread and gave thanks and gave it to them. Their eyes were opened and they recognized him. But he vanished from their sight.

They said to one another, Did not our hearts burn within us as he spoke to us on the way and opened to us the Scripture.

In that very hour they rose up and returned to Jerusalem and found the eleven and those who were with them, who said,

The Lord indeed is risen and has appeared to Simon. Then they began to rehearse the things which had happened on the way and how he was made known to them in the breaking of bread.

Section 188. JESUS APPEARS TO THE DISCIPLES

Luke 24:36-43.   John 20:19-25

It was late on that first day of the week, and the doors were shut where the disciples were for fear of the Jews.

While they were speaking of these things, Jesus came and stood among them and said, Peace be with you.

They were terrified and afraid, supposing that they saw a spirit.

He said to them, why are you agitated?   and why do doubts arise in your hearts?   Look at my hands and my feet, that it is I myself.   Handle me and see, for a spirit does not have flesh and bones as you see that I have.

When he had said this, he showed them his hands and his side.

While they still did not believe from joy and marveled, he said to them, Have you any food here?

They gave him a piece of broiled fish.   Taking it, he ate it before them.   Then the disciples rejoiced when they saw that it was the Lord.

Jesus said to them again, Peace be with you!   as the Father sent me, so send I you.   Having said this, he breathed upon them and said, Receive the Holy Spirit.   Whose sins you forgive, they have been forgiven them.   Whose you hold they have been held.

Thomas, one of the twelve, called the Twin, was not with them when Jesus came.

When the other disciples told him, We have seen the Lord; he said to them, Except I shall see in his hands the print of the nails and put my finger into the print of the nails and thrust my hand into his side, I will not believe.

Section 189. Jesus Appears to Apostles with Thomas Present

John 20:26-29

After eight days, the disciples were again inside and Thomas with them. The doors were closed, but Jesus came and stood among them and said, Peace be with you.

Then he said to Thomas, Reach your finger here and see my hands; reach out your hand and thrust it in my side; and be not an unbeliever but a believer.

Thomas said to him, My Lord and my God.

Jesus said to him, Because you have seen me, do you believe? Blessed are those who believe though they do not see.

Section 190. Appearance by the Sea of Galilee

John 21

After these things, Jesus revealed himself again to the disciples by the Sea of Tiberius; he revealed himself like this.

Simon Peter and Thomas, who is called the Twin, and Nathanael from Cana of Galilee, the sons of Zebedee, and two others of his disciples were together.

Simon Peter said to them, I am going fishing.

They said to him, We are going with you.

They went out and entered into the boat. During the night, they caught nothing.

Just as day was dawning, Jesus stood on the beach; yet the disciples did not know that it was Jesus. He said to them, Children, you have no fish, do you?

They answered, No.

He said to them, Cast the net on the right side of the boat and you will find some.

So they cast and could no longer draw it in because of the multitude of fishes. That disciple whom Jesus loved said to Peter, It is the Lord.

When Simon Peter heard that it was the Lord, he put his coat about him (for he was naked), and dived into the sea. But the other disciples came in the boat (for they were not far from the shore, about a hundred yards), pulling the net full of fishes. When they came out on the shore, they saw a fire of charcoal laid with fish lying on it and bread. Jesus said to them, Bring some of the fish which you have caught.

Simon Peter went up and drew the net ashore full of great fishes—one hundred and fifty three. In spite of there being so many, the net did not break.

Jesus said to them, Come and have breakfast.

None of the disciples dared to inquire of him, Who are you? For they knew that it was the Lord.

Jesus came and took bread and gave it to them and likewise with the fish.

This was the third time that Jesus had revealed himself to the disciples after he arose from the dead.

When they had eaten, Jesus said to Simon Peter, Simon, son of John, are you devoted[3] to me more than to these?

---

3. A play of words is undoubtedly involved here. The distinction between *phileo* (warm personal affection) and *agapso* (unselfish devotion to one's interests) is not always maintained in the New Testament. But such changing from one to the other in the same context is certainly not without meaning. Thus Jesus is drawing a deliberate contrast between the intelligent and unselfish devotion which he demands and the personal affection which Peter gives. It matters not that the Aramaic which they spoke has no words for this distinction, the thought must be supposed to have been preserved by John.

He said, Yes, Lord, you know that I love you.

He said to him, Feed my lambs.

He said to him again the second time, Simon, son of John, Are you devoted to me?

He said to him, Yes, Lord, you know that I love you.

He said to him, Tend to my sheep.

He said to him a third time, Simon, son of John, do you really love me?

Peter was grieved that he said to him the third time, Do you love me? He said, Lord, you know all things, you know that I love you.

Jesus said to him, Feed my sheep. Truly, truly, I tell you when you were young, you dressed yourself and walked where you wished. When you grow old, you will stretch out your hands, and others will dress you and lead you where you do not wish.

This he said signifying by what kind of death he would glorify God.

Having said this, he said to him, Follow me.

Peter turned and saw the disciple whom Jesus loved following, (he who had leaned upon his breast at the supper and said, Lord, who will betray you?) and said to Jesus, Lord, what of this one?

Jesus said to him, If I want him to remain until I come, what is that to you? Follow me.

Therefore this report went out to the brethren that that disciple would not die. But Jesus did not say of him that he would not die, but, If I want him to remain till I come, what is that to you?

This is the disciple who testifies of these things and has written these things, and we know that his testimony is true.

Section 191. APPEARANCE IN THE MOUNTAINS OF GALILEE

Matthew 28:16-20

The eleven disciples went to Galilee, to the mountain which Jesus had appointed them, and when they saw him, they worshipped him, but some doubted.

When Jesus had come to them, he said, All authority was given to me in heaven and on earth. Go therefore, and make disciples of all nations, baptizing them in the name of the Father and of the Son and of the Holy Spirit, teaching them to practice all things which I have commanded you. And, lo, I am with you always, until the end of the age.

Section 192. PARTING INSTRUCTIONS OF THE SAVIOUR

Luke 24:44-49

He said to them, These are my words which I have spoken to you, being still with you, for all the things written in the law of Moses and in the prophets and in the Psalms about me must be fulfilled. Then he opened their minds to understand the scriptures, and said to them, Thus it is written that the Messiah should suffer and be raised the third day from the dead, so that repentance and forgiveness of sins should be preached in his name to all the nations, beginning from Jerusalem. You are witnesses of these things. And lo, I send the promise of my Father upon you. Stay in the city until you are clothed with power from on high.

Section 193. THE ASCENSION NEAR BETHANY

Luke 24:50-53

Then he led them out to Bethany, and lifting up his hands, he blessed them. As he blessed them, he parted from them and was carried into heaven. They, worshipping him, returned to Jerusalem with great joy, and were continually in the temple praising God.